SURGICAL PRAYER

Tom Deuschle

Celebration Ministries International
Harare, Zimbabwe

Surgical Prayer
Published by:
Kingdom Celebration Media
P.O. Box HG88
Highlands, Harare,
Zimbabwe
ISBN 0-9817935-0-9

Printed in the United States of America.

Dedication

It has been a real challenge to attempt to take the life of our church and ministry and condense it onto the pages of this book. This revelation has given our church and many people in it breakthrough, and has proven to be a benchmark teaching and a pillar in the foundation of the call and vision of our church, which is centered in establishing the reformation vision. As we apply surgical prayer to our lives, it will not only break the bonds and operation of iniquitous thinking in our lives, but will allow the release of the purpose of God in individuals, families, churches and nations. I thank God for this revelation and have received it with joy and gratitude. It has touched hundreds of lives powerfully, so I pass it on to you without reservation.

For her phenomenal support of my vision I thank my remarkable wife and prophet to our vision, Bonnie. You are not only the most beautiful woman in the world, and an incredible mother to our five awesome children, but have also willingly taken up mentoring our spiritual family as well. You are the most passionate worship director and leader I know, but above all it's your fierce drive to bring us all into the things of God, and your willingness to release all that God has given you for us, for which I honor you and am deeply grateful.

My sons, Tommy, a man of God in his own right, Jonathan psalmist extraordinaire, Benjamin, son of my right hand, Daniel, I see the God's healing power is in you, and my precious daughter, beautiful worshipful Sarah, I love you all and thank God in my every remembrance of you.

To our devoted and dedicated prayer leader, Pastor Nicky Ferreira and all of the Domain Prayer leaders, thank you, well done good and faithful servants, keep growing from strength to strength in this the day of our battle. May you find many willing to come alongside and join you in realizing our vision of Building People, Building Dreams, and Transforming Lives and Reforming Nations.

Special thanks to Gillian Spurway, who gave of her heart and time to help put this manuscript together. Through the entire process you have been amazing. And to the host of supporters and helpers in the process, more numerous than can be named in this dedication, but who are known by all of us who have labored, and more importantly, who are known by God, thank you.

To our powerful church family, I exhort you as Celebration Churches worldwide to continue to increase, to bring restoration and influence in your God-given spheres of influence. Continue taking dominion and establishing the Kingdom of God in your domains, which is righteousness—right thinking, peace and joy in the Holy Ghost. Stand firm, rejoice in the Lord always, pray without ceasing, and in everything give thanks . . ., "owe nothing to anyone except to love one another, for he who loves his neighbor has fulfilled the law" (Romans 13:8).

The Deuschle family
From Left to Right: Daniel, Pastor Tom, Tommy, Pastor Bonnie,
Sarah, Benjamin, and Jonathan

Contents

Dedication

Foreword

Introduction

PART ONE: A TRANSFORMED PRAYER LIFE

1. Why "Surgical" Prayer?.................................1

2. Spheres of Influence 7

PART TWO: PRINCIPLES FOR TRANSFORMATION

3. Surgical Prayer is Precise 37

4. Surgical Prayer is Penetrating.................49

5. Surgical Prayer is Purposeful 81

PART THREE: PATTERNS FOR TRANSFORMATION

6. Surgical Prayer is Prescriptive.............103

7. Surgical Prayer is Prophetic 125

8. Surgical Prayer is Pastoral...................141

9. Surgical Prayer is Practical..................155

10. Conclusion 169

Significant Statements

Foreword

As founder of the International House of Prayer in Kansas City, the subject of prayer and how Jesus will engage His Bride, the Church, has been the passion of my life in God. However, I have known many dry and unanointed prayer times. I found a place of common ground as I read the preface to my friend, Tom Deuschle's book, as he was transparent about how difficult and even boring prayer can be, yet he knew how important it was to God, and therefore, how important it should be to him. I appreciated this insight, as I have come to the same conclusion in my life.

Jesus the Bridegroom God will not come back until the Church worldwide is immersed in prayer, crying out for His return. The Holy Spirit is raising up a global prayer and worship movement that will cry out for His return (Revelation 22:17).

Pastor Tom Deuschle's revelation of the Kingdom is based on daily prayer that has been established in his congregation in Harare, Zimbabwe, as well as his numerous church plants around the globe. This book relates the journey of one man, in Zimbabwe, Africa which has just recently been deemed by the United Nations (UN) as a "failed nation." As you can imagine, it takes a lot to get this rating by the UN.

How do you survive in a nation that:

a. Has two million percent inflation

b. Has 80% unemployment in the nation

c. Has an HIV/Aids infection rate of over 30%

d. Has an average life expectancy of only 34 years old

You do it by revelation…you move from worship to wisdom to revelation…and by inspiration of the Holy Spirit for daily prayer.

In a congregation of over 17,000 people in Harare alone and hundreds of church plants in Africa (South Africa, Zimbabwe, Mozambique) and in England, they have endured the harshest of environments and self funded a 150,000 square foot facility that would be considered a first class facility in any nation.

In addition, the facility is primarily self funded by the members, and has no debt!

The facility took 14 years to build (seven years to buy the land and seven years to build the facility).

How do you endure this journey? By prayer! *Surgical Prayer* is a strategy that God released to Tom as the war in Iraq escalated. The Lord impressed upon his spirit the scripture that says that, "the natural world mirrors the supernatural" and that our prayers could be very precise and surgical in their effectiveness, if we understood the power of this strategy in prayer.

Bunker Buster Prayer is another strategy the Lord released to Tom, again related to the war in Iraq. Those powerful prayers that can go deep and penetrate strongholds in all spheres of influence: personal, family, business, education, arts, spiritual/church affairs, and the affairs of government.

In my meetings with Tom, I recognized the gift of wisdom and revelation that has been released to him, by the

Holy Spirit, in one of the harshest environments on the planet, and yet he has embraced the revelation given in prayer, that the Kingdom of God is right thinking, peace and joy in the Holy Spirit....that the Kingdom is a disposition...not a place...and that this place can be powerfully accessed by prayer, giving us direction to recapture dominion in our sphere of influence.

It is my sincere desire that you would read this book...and be challenged by the insights.

It is my sincere belief that Jesus, the Bridegroom, is coming back to planet earth, for His Bride, the global Church, as she cries out in a global concert of prayer around the earth. I am moved by Tom Deuschle's heart to minister, in day and night prayer, for the Bridegroom to come and touch every sphere of influence, in one of the harshest places on the earth. I am sure your heart will be moved, as well, as you read of their journey, and how "Surgical Prayer" released the revelation and power of the Kingdom of God to them.

Mike Bickle
International House of Prayer
Kansas City, Missouri
www.IHOP.org

Introduction

I was just about to attend another of our many prayer meetings in the church, and was feeling nauseous; I couldn't understand why something so powerful for so many, and so beautiful for some, was such drudgery for me. In spite of the fact that I was pastoring a growing congregation of more than 3,000 members at this time, and was encouraging people to pray and intercede for all kinds of things, I still dreaded our corporate prayer meetings. My teaching on prayer was sound and the principles of prayer were fully understood. In fact our prayer meetings were well attended by most church standards, with between 50 to 100 people attending twice a week, on a Friday morning and a Monday night, as well as many intermittent and unscheduled times of prayer both in and out of the church.

Part of my dilemma as pastor was watching those I had encouraged to attend prayer meetings become increasingly disillusioned with prayer. I'd watch and listen as the different members of our congregation poured out their hearts to God about needs felt, perceived, real and urgent. All of the prayers were important to God and the person praying, but they all seemed so disconnected. A housewife would pour out her heart to God regarding the educational needs of her children and the children of the nation, or a farmer appeal for God's intervention so he and his family would not be removed from their farm, whilst the business people of the church would stand by waiting to have their chance. Their burden was to address the Lord, and secure the agreement of the corporate gathering, for the national needs of commerce and industry that was under the attack of sinister forces of corruption and graft.

I consoled myself with the fact that we should be able to wait on the needs of other people even if it had no relevance to our situation, and I exhorted those who attended to be patient while prayers that were not of interest and in their circle of need or influence were being offered to the Lord. The problem was that certain needs stirred my spirit and struck a chord in my heart, while other prayers put me to sleep and quite frankly were of little or no interest to me or many of those I had assembled to pray.

At one point I thought that praying in tongues might solve this dilemma, so for a while we just spoke in tongues for the hour. I tried to convince myself that this was really being effective, but whether we prayed in our understanding, each one alternately speaking out our heartfelt concerns, or spoke in tongues corporately, the desperation within me mounted. With the vision of reformation pounding through my spirit, and pressure mounting from the escalating needs of a nation being torn apart by political unrest, corruption, economic upheaval, and disillusionment, I cried out, "God this is so ineffective!"

In the midst of this uneasy and agitated scenario, during an especially anointed Sunday morning service, I heard myself prophesying. I declared that there would be an increase in prayer in our church, and to cater for it we would pray on a daily basis. So our intercessors went into action and began daily prayer meetings. Now, this had to either be God, or ignorance gone to seed!

Multiplying what wasn't working and expecting a different result is foolishness. I attended for one week and knew that either I had to change, or our prayer meetings had to change.

Since that time I have seen lack-lustre, misled and misdirected prayer turn into the driving force behind a movement for reformation in our nation. I'm convinced that the principles and precepts that are laid out in the pages of this book will prove to be invaluable to those who are struggling with corporate prayer as I did. May the Holy Spirit help you to lay hold of these practical and effective keys that have transformed my prayer life and have changed large numbers of my church members into a forceful army of intelligent, focused and surgically sharp intercessors.

This book is the story of the changes that took place in me and consequently in the prayer ministry. We are now seeing the effect in our church, our families, our businesses and the nation.

PART ONE

A Transformed Prayer Life

"The greatest will he be of
reformers and apostles,
who can set the Church to praying."

Martin Luther

Chapter 1
Why "Surgical" Prayer?

Why another book on prayer? After all, there is already a plethora of information and books on prayer. Through the years I have been bombarded with prayer books, prayer seminars, prayer workshops, instructions on prayer walking, prayer mapping, the 10/40 window — the list is endless. Although I could see tremendous value in the truths contained in all this material, only a handful of people, in my church, were responding to the prayer concepts put forward. Why was this? This question would eventually lead me to change the way I think and feel about prayer, and eventually write what you are reading in this book.

Zimbabwe

I saw that as Zimbabwe, the nation I had chosen to serve God in, went through seasons of drought, political unrest and economic recession, people were stirred to pray more. The greater the social upheaval the more intense was our desire to pray. Prayer increased within our church, within the city and within the nation, in direct proportion to the perceived and real needs. However, as soon as there was a return to some semblance of normality, prayer meetings dwindled in number to a few faithful intercessors. There seemed to be no prolonged strategy of prayer that could sustain a quorum.

1

My frustration mounted, fueled by so many unfocused prayer meetings, driving me to seek the Lord. What follows in the next few chapters is the strategy I believe God gave me.

Why "Surgical" Prayer? This was God's response to my desperation with our erratic corporate prayer. It describes the strategy for our church's growth in kingdom prayer and came as I was watching an international news report talking about surgical air-strikes. The presenter described and compared the use of smart bombs, with what he referred to as, "dumb bombs" and "carpet bombing". The whole emphasis centered around how this new technology worked and how the resultant outcome was a phenomenal improvement in successful strike rate. The reporter said something that radically changed my life, "These bombs have surgical accuracy. We now live in the day of surgical warfare. We can go in and surgically remove one person and leave the rest of the civilian population untouched." I was overawed at how warfare had developed, and as I continued watching, I heard God say to me, "That's what I want in prayer — surgical accuracy." The realization dawned on me of how often we have wielded a broad sword in prayer, instead of a sharp, precise surgical instrument.

Again a few years later, I was watching a television program explaining how people had learned to build deeper bunkers to escape the smart bombs. I wondered how technology could possibly overcome this new defense. Almost as soon as my query arose, the presenter went on to describe a new smart bomb, which they called a "bunker buster", devised especially to deal with these deep bunkers. A bunker-buster is a bomb weighing between 500-900 kilograms that uses smart bomb technology, which makes it surgically accurate, but with the power to destroy an underground bunker. Once again I heard God say, "I want to teach the church how to pray "bunker-buster" prayers, prayers which are both accurate and powerful.

A skilled surgeon will take a surgical instrument, like a scalpel, and use it carefully and deliberately in the service of healing. That same scalpel in unskilled hands could cause untold injury and damage.

Prayer, like the smart bomb, when directed with purpose and intent, will always hit the mark, just as the scalpel in the hand of a surgeon will bring about precise and intended results.

In contrast to smart bombs or skilled surgery, many of our corporate prayer meetings comprised groups of individuals, each praying for their perception of the prayer needs of the church, city or nation, or for their own personal needs, and expecting others to listen and agree with them. The effect was the difference between a shotgun blast and the shot of a sniper, between a carpet bomb and a smart bomb, or a bunker-buster. I now appreciated why I was frustrated with our non-directed prayer meetings, and was prepared to receive a blueprint for expansion of our corporate prayer.

Building People Building Dreams, Transforming Lives Reforming Nations

Our strategy rolled out into what we now call "Kingdom" or "domain" prayer. This strategy focuses on *twelve* domains or spheres of influence in our society, which I will elaborate on in the chapters to come. My intention was to empower the vision of our church, which is *"building people, building dreams; transforming lives, reforming nations"*, thus making prayer more practical and contagious. I wanted to see the whole congregation influenced not just the intercessors and pastors.

The early reformer, Martin Luther, once said, "If the Gospel does not address issues of the day, then it is no Gospel at all." His statement echoes our desire and mandate to address the issues of the day with the power of the Gospel. In the Great Commission Jesus gave us the commandment "to preach the Gospel to every creature…and disciple all nations" (Mark 16:15, Matthew 24:14, Matthew 28:19,20).

God was calling our church to a new season, a new strategy and a new level of corporate prayer, that had to be matched with bold, biblical action. He was giving us new keys and ideas, as to how we could mobilize and multiply more people to pray intentionally and powerfully; people who were determined to live by conviction, based on biblical pattern and principle, in each of the *domains*.

God was challenging and reminding all of us that the goal of the church and missions worldwide is not just salvation of souls and global evangelism, but it is to disciple and impact nations with the *Gospel of the Kingdom of God* in every sphere of life. God had given me a mandate to build a church, a family of believers, that would bring about transformation and reformation in Africa and affect the world, starting in Zimbabwe. In order to accomplish this in the context in which we found ourselves, our church congregation would need to challenge and change the increasing corruption, hopelessness, deep-seated cultural mind-sets and lifestyles that Zimbabwe and Africa were facing. This meant we were going to have to both work out that change within ourselves and also adjust our focus.

God had already given our church congregation a prophetic and apostolic mandate to be a "house of prayer for all nations" (Isaiah 56:7). It was time to move from being a growing, influential church with only a few seasoned intercessors to becoming a strategic, praying church body that was aggressively and effectively influencing all spheres of life, not just spiritually, but visibly and practically. It was time for the Church and its members to be living witnesses in the market-place; it was time to shake the salt from the salt shaker. We could no longer afford the luxury, or should I say deception, of being one thing in the Church and something different in the world. I say deception because this divided reality produces powerless and deluded lives, unable and in truth unwilling, to influence anyone or anything for the Kingdom of God.

I knew that God was calling us to rediscover the power and influence of His Kingdom Gospel through a bold, new *Kingdom Prayer* strategy that would affect every area of society, not just the Church. We had seen and experienced God's supernatural provision in the 1990's and early part of the new millennium, as we had actively pursued the principles of prosperity and were able to build and pay cash for our world-class, 150,000 square- foot, church building. Although this was a fourteen year ordeal, our congregation and many of our key business people prospered as they applied God's principles of faith, first fruits, tithing and Kingdom stewardship, and saw their own businesses established as they first built God's House. The irony was that while we were building, growing and prospering as a church, Zimbabwe as a nation, was in the middle of chaos. She was suffering her most severe drought, which, combined with unstable political and critical economic conditions, was compounded only by the ever-increasing HIV and AIDS pandemic.

I realized that not only was Zimbabwe facing disaster in every social domain, but the majority of traditional and evangelical churches in the nation were still deeply divided, racially and, politically, as well as denominationally.

The situation demanded we take greater dominion and authority in the many areas of life we had previously abdicated or ignored. It was not enough to just pray. We needed more truth and definitely more action. In spite of the mounting hardships Zimbabwe was facing, the economic meltdown, scorning and sanctions by the European Union (EU), the United States and the International Monetary Fund (IMF), as well as the ever mounting HIV and AIDS and orphan statistics, God wanted to do something extraordinary in Zimbabwe. Although it seemed we had been forgotten by the outside world and surrounding nations; God had Zimbabwe right in the forefront.

The media and news reports were anything but positive. An aggressive land reform exercise yielded nothing but chaos, large scale hunger and unemployment. There was a mass exodus of Zimbabweans of all races, to pastures thought to be "greener" or at least safer. The country was struggling under the burden of escalating inflation moving from 500% to an estimated 2 million% and climbing inflation, 80% unemployment, the health and banking sectors on the brink of virtual collapse, a 30% HIV and AIDS infection rate, and over one million children orphaned and destitute. If there ever was a "such a time as this" for God to intervene and deliver a nation, it was now.

It was in this context that God spoke to me about raising up apostolic people from the key sectors of the nation with a biblical world view, radical faith in His promises and principles, and a passion and purpose to influence every sphere of life with the Kingdom of God.

Chapter 2
Spheres of Influence

God's reformation process is returning power to the Church. One of the keys to reformation is changing our mind-sets and transforming our world views. As Christians we have every reason for winning the battle for the hearts and minds of the people of the world and "possessing the nations as our inheritance" (Psalm 2:8 NKJV), but we must use God's Kingdom weapons to wage war and not those of the world.

The weapons we fight with are not the weapons of the world [God has given them to us]. **On the contrary, they have divine power to demolish strongholds.**

We [must first expose, then] **demolish** [all] **arguments** [philosophies, ideas, theories, lies, worldviews] **and every pretension that sets itself up against the knowledge of God, and we take captive every thought to make it obedient to Christ.** **2 Corinthians 10:4,5 (NIV)**

Do not be conformed to this world this age, [fashioned after and adapted to its external, superficial customs]. But be transformed (changed) by the [entire] renewal of your mind [by its new ideals and attitude], so that you may prove [for yourselves] what is the good and acceptable and perfect will of God, *even* **the thing that is good and acceptable and perfect [in His sight for you].** **Romans 12:2 (AMP)**

In our desire to see a biblical world view and Kingdom reformation advance in Africa we knew we must begin to think and act like God in relation to all spheres of society. So many Christians today suffer from "split personalities". Their lives are divided into compartments: the "religious" or sacred, what they do, like attending church or a prayer meeting or a Bible Study, etc.; and the "secular", their jobs, recreation, and even education. Much of this "evangelical Gnosticism" is what has opened the doors in the West to an increased popularity of New Age Mysticism and the fascination with Islam.

What is Truth?

A pastor friend of mine lamented the fact that many people in the Church have moved from hypocrisy to duplicity, especially in America. He feels that this accelerated when Bill Clinton was President of the United States. It became generally accepted by the U.S. public and the world, that what a man did in private did not have to match what he did in public. When our behavior in life is inconsistent with what we do in church or public office, we are duplicitous. Until this duplicitous thinking is dealt with in the church, we will be no better off than our contemporaries in the world. Herein lies the challenge; we need to integrate what we pray with what we think, feel and speak outside of our prayer meetings. Prayer in the church should change from an activity that we do, to a way of life. This is the essence of transformation.

Jesus is the perfect example of someone who was expressing the Kingdom in the duplicitous society of the Roman Empire in the occupied territory of Israel. As Jesus stood before Pontius Pilate, who had determined to have nothing to do with this matter at the behest of his wife, as well as wrestling with his own conscience, he asks a very profound question, that reveals his own duplicity.

So Pilate came out to them and asked, "What charges are you bringing against this man?"

"If he were not a criminal," they replied, "we would not have handed him over to you."

Pilate said, "Take him yourselves and judge him by your own law." "But we have no right to execute anyone," the Jews objected.

This happened so that the words Jesus had spoken indicating the kind of death he was going to die would be fulfilled.

Pilate then went back inside the palace, summoned Jesus and asked him, "Are you the king of the Jews?"

"Is that your own idea," Jesus asked, "or did others talk to you about me?"

"Am I a Jew?" Pilate replied. "It was your people and your chief priests who handed you over to me. What is it you have done?"

Jesus said, "My kingdom is not of this world. If it were, my servants would fight to prevent my arrest by the Jews. But now my kingdom is from another place."

"You are a king, then!" said Pilate. Jesus answered, "You are right in saying I am a king. In fact, for this reason I was born, and for this I came into the world, to testify to the truth. Everyone on the side of truth listens to me."

"What is truth?" Pilate asked. With this he went out again to the Jews and said, "I find no basis for a charge against him."

                                        John 18:29-38 (NIV)

Jesus is very direct with Pilate, He says, *"Everyone on the side of truth listens to me"*. What an indictment on Pilate, but Jesus' comment may be no different to us today! This is becoming an awkward and often challenging question for duplicitous people to answer, "what is truth?" The more the Church becomes duplicitous, the harder it is to have commandments and truth as foundations. Even today in the West, many of our evangelical churches are following some denominational churches, down a path where previously accepted values and morals, are being ignored, rejected and discarded. Instead of being a voice of change we have become echoes in a secular, humanist society.

Transformational Development: A Dynamic Process

Transformational development is a dynamic process. Societies change only as far as the individuals in them change, and nations are discipled one person at a time, from the inside out. Lasting change begins with the preaching of the Gospel and involves the exchange of false ideologies and opposing world views for a biblical world view, which is the truth.

God's intention from the beginning was, that not only individuals, but families, tribes, cultures and nations be redeemed and reformed to reflect His goodness and glory.

In order to accomplish this great task there must be an overarching framework and understanding of the process. An effective strategy for prayer or reformation will address issues that affect nations as well as those which affect churches and individuals. In other words, in order for the principles and patterns to work they must be universal in application.

As we endeavor to transform and disciple a nation, there are many steps in the process. We begin with preaching the Gospel of the Kingdom, in other words we challenge world views. This results in repentant souls and regenerated lives, the basis for real change. Once the inward change has occurred we begin teaching the foundations of Biblical world view, and engage in the process of renewing our minds to God's principles and patterns, resulting in reformed lives, marriages and families. Only after this groundwork is in place, are we in a position to begin to challenge the status quo and exercise dominion in the various spheres of society we find ourselves engaged in. This pattern then repeats itself in the lives of individuals that we are involved with and eventually results in a transformed society, a discipled nation and a reformed culture. Any lesser goal than discipling the nation is to forfeit Christ's commission:

> **Go then and make disciples of all the nations, baptizing them into the name of the Father and of the Son and of the Holy Spirit,**
>
> **teaching them to observe everything that I have commanded you, and lo, I am with you all the days, (perpetually, uniformly and on every occasion) to the [very] close and consumption of the age. Amen [even] [so let it be].** **Matthew 28:19,20 (AMP)**

When God gave me the concept of *Kingdom prayer*, I came to the understanding that there were spheres of influence in society, that we referred to as "domains", where deliberate and specific prayer could make a difference. Hence the name *domain prayer* was adopted by the church to describe this kind of praying. Why domain prayer? Because the Lord's original intention for mankind, was for a divine purpose, to have dominion.

> **God said, Let Us [Father, Son, and Holy Spirit] make mankind in Our image, after Our likeness and let them have *complete authority* over the fish of the sea, the birds of the air, the [tame] beasts, and over all of the earth, and over every thing that creeps upon the earth.**

11

> **And God blessed them and said to them, Be fruitful, multiply, and fill the earth and subdue it [with using all its vast resources]; and have *dominion* over the fish of the sea, the birds of the air, and over every living creature that moves upon the earth.**
>
> **Genesis 1:26,28 (AMP)**

> **You made him to have *dominion* over the works of Your hands;...**
>
> **Psalm 8:6 (AMP)**

Dominion is an important aspect, for without an understanding of this kind of thinking we will be ineffective in our attempts to affect change by prayer or in practice. We must understand that in the primary sense of what we are commissioned to do on earth, it has to do with God's Kingdom and His dominion and our relationship to His Kingdom.

Jesus taught us to pray, *"Your Kingdom come, Your will be done on earth as it is in heaven"* (Matthew 6:10 NIV). What is the Kingdom? It is the rule of God on earth. This requires us to both understand and submit to God as King of heaven and earth. The Kingdom is the King's domain — any place where the King has rule. As we acknowledge, receive and submit to God's authority in our own personal lives, this in turn begins to emanate to every sphere in which we function.

I visualized people's interest being provoked by at least one of the domains, and it was my desire to see their passion being aroused so they would focus on pursuing dominion in their various spheres of influence. I am aware that there are a multitude of different spheres, but in setting forth our strategy I narrowed our focus to twelve domains that we see as having the greatest influence in society.

In an attempt to be efficient we combined related domains and assigned them to specific days of the week, where we would gather corporately to focus our prayers.

Domain Prayer Schedule
6:30 am to 7:30 am (Monday-Friday)

DAY	DOMAIN
Monday	Business, Economics, Agriculture
Tuesday	Church, Government
Wednesday	Family, Education
Thursday	Health, Science & Technology
Friday	Arts & Media, Entertainment & Sports

Although I felt God had given me the plan for domain prayer, I wasn't prepared for the impact and the effect it would produce. When we came together in our domains, we experienced the power of purpose. As we all focused on the same thing, and agreed as touching one thing, we witnessed a tangible increase in the intensity of God's power, and answers to our prayers. We were being overwhelmed by testimonies of those who were receiving answers to their prayers. God's presence was becoming more evident in our areas of influence and His power was being released through our lives as we continued in the process of learning to effectively use this revelation.

Five-Fold Ministry in the Marketplace

An integral part of this dynamic which we have encouraged is the expression of the five-fold ministry in each domain, recognizing apostles, prophets, evangelists, pastors and teachers in each sphere.

This may seem foreign, especially to those who see the church as an ecclesiastical body, or a hierarchical system. From my vantage point I see every member supplying something to the whole. "In the past in some circles, our approach to church not only did not support the idea of workplace ministry, we even shamed some business people and professionals for being in the world. We've had the approach that, "if you're not a preacher or serving in the ministry, or on the mission field, you are really not doing the work of the ministry." The times have changed. I realized that many of my top leaders in the church were also very successful in the marketplace. Instead of trying to get them to stop marketplace ministry, I recognized them as ministry gifts for the church to equip the saints for the work of the ministry in the marketplace using real marketplace strategies.

This was a bit scary as it meant I was out of a job, other than to train the trainers, but the dynamic has built a base of leaders that can go anywhere in any domain and be powerful witnesses for the Gospel and be voices of reform and transformation wherever they go.

Daniel and Joseph were both raised in cultures without a biblical world view and were used to transform nations with opposing, hostile world views. Although Daniel and Joseph were educated in the cultures in which they were captive, they did not acquiesce to those cultures. Daniel sat at the king's table, but did not partake of the king's food. God gave both of these men wisdom, understanding, knowledge and favor with the people of those cultures. Eventually their godly wisdom led them to be architects of reformation in blatantly pagan nations.

We must ask God for the same wisdom, keys and revelation in order to bring the Kingdom of God's rule and reign into our own personal lives and our respective nations. As we engage a world swept up in an information age, where it appears that more and more knowledge is available to anyone, we will not convince people of anything through mere knowledge. What the Church has to offer is unique and given to us by God. We have access to wisdom from above. The world is not having an information problem, but a wisdom problem. The Church has an opportunity to give real answers to the world using a source that is inaccessible to the world, the wisdom of God.

This wisdom descendeth not from above, but is earthly, sensual, devilish.

For where envying and strife is, there is confusion and every evil work.

But the wisdom that is from above is first pure, then peaceable, gentle, and easy to be intreated, full of mercy and good fruits, without partiality, and without hypocrisy." **James 3:15-17 (KJV)**

When we choose to engage in Kingdom rule there are positive, identifiable consequences. If we neglect Kingdom rule there are also negative, identifiable consequences.

What is Meant by the Kingdom of God and Kingdom Rule?

I think at this juncture it is important that we understand precisely what is meant by the Kingdom of God and Kingdom rule. Often when this topic is raised in the Church, people think of a physical kingdom that somehow looks like one of our natural governments on earth, or is in fact going to replace natural governments on earth. Although the Kingdom of God influences natural governments, it is more a disposition than it is a structured government.

Let me explain. First of all, the Scripture declares that, "the Kingdom of God comes without observation, it is in the hearts of men" (Luke 17:20 NIV). Jesus said, "the Kingdom of God is within you" (Luke 17:21 NIV). So if it's "within us" and it is "without observation", then in that regard its entirely different to natural kingdoms or governments. The apostle Paul qualifies this even further when he says that, "for the kingdom of God is not eating and drinking, but it is righteousness peace and joy in the Holy Spirit" (Romans 14:17 NIV).

Righteous here is the Aramaic word, *dikaios*, meaning equitable in character and action, derived from right principles and decisions, or simply put, *right-thinking*.

Notice from this verse that two thirds of the Kingdom has to do with our emotions, *peace* and *joy*. The other third has to do with our thought life. That is why I say that the Kingdom of God is a disposition, not a destination. What God is saying is that if we will choose to live in His Kingdom, which is right-thinking (righteousness), peace and joy, we will not have the effects on our lives of the kingdom of darkness. The kingdom of darkness is accompanied by equally powerful emotions and thoughts, albeit they are in the negative realm such as fear, doubt, anxiousness, bitterness, etcetera.

For some this is a foreign idea, especially those who have been taught in prayer, that we are warring against some physical kingdom. I am not denying the fact that there are many manifestations of evil and that there are many evil people and ideas that must be resisted physically, which God has appointed the authorities to deal with, "For rulers hold no terror for those who do right, but for those who do wrong...he is God's servant, an agent of wrath to bring punishment on the wrong doer.... The authorities are God's servants..." (Romans 13:3,4,6 NIV). In my experience, the greatest warfare I ever face is trying to stay in right thinking, peace and joy, when those around me are in insanity, distress and fear.

As we begin to study surgical prayer, it is important that we realize from what mindset we must pray. We are either praying from "in-the-Kingdom" or we're praying from a position "out-of-the-Kingdom". Which prayers do you suppose get answered?

You are jealous *and* covet [what others have] and your Desires go unfulfilled; [so] you become murderers. [To hate is to murder as far as your hearts are concerned.] You burn with envy and anger and are not able to obtain [the gratification, the contentment and the happiness that you seek], so you fight and war. You do not have because you do not ask.

[Or] you do ask [God for them] and yet fail to receive, because you ask with wrong purpose and evil, selfish motives. Your intention is, [when you get what you desire] you spend it in sensual pleasures.

James 4:2,3 (AMP)

Many of the prayers I've heard through the years, are prayed from a position of fear, anxiety, anger, even judgment, as well as many other negative thoughts and emotions. These prayers in fact, do not constitute prayers of the Kingdom. God cannot honor fear, doubt, anxiety or for that matter any negative emotion. The guidelines for His Kingdom are for us to remain and abide in the fruit of the Spirit. For in that rarified atmosphere God hears, and answers prayer.

We can all think of many examples especially in corporate prayer meetings, where prayers were being prayed at people, or to correct circumstances, or even to vent anger or frustration at governments or principalities. Unfortunately, although these prayers often sounded powerful, they are being prayed from a wrong spirit. They were not Kingdom prayers.

The Kingdom Elements of Prayer

We've experienced horrific conditions; economically, medically, and politically in the nation of Zimbabwe. Even under these harsh conditions in the country, it's hard to compare them to the pressure the early church felt under Roman rule and Jewish scorn. Yet when they had been persecuted and beaten for preaching the Gospel, we see a Kingdom prayer usher from their spirits in a corporate prayer meeting, that literally "rocks the house."

When they heard this, they raised their voices together in prayer to God. "Sovereign Lord," they said, "you made the heaven and the earth and the sea, and everything in them.

You spoke by the Holy Spirit through the mouth of your servant, our father David: "Why do the nations rage and the peoples plot in vain?

The kings of the earth take their stand and the rulers gather together against the Lord and against his Anointed One.

Indeed Herod and Pontius Pilate met together with the Gentiles and the people of Israel in this city to conspire against your holy servant Jesus, whom you anointed.

They did what your power and will had decided beforehand should happen.

Now, Lord, consider their threats and enable your servants to speak your word with great boldness.

Stretch out your hand to heal and perform miraculous signs and wonders through the name of your holy servant Jesus."

After they prayed, the place where they were meet-ing was shaken. And they were all filled with the Holy Spirit and spoke the word of God boldly.

Acts 4:24-31 (NIV)

Notice just a few of the Kingdom elements of this prayer.

First of all, notice how the opening mirrors the way Jesus taught them to pray as recorded in Matthew 6:9-13. They prayed to the Father, the maker of Heaven and earth.

Next they begin to affirm kingdom rule, declaring what the Kingdom in heaven looks like, not the situation on earth, reminding God of His Word.

Notice when it comes to the judgments against them, they ask God to consider their enemies' threats, which is a form of forgiveness and instead of asking for them to be bound or destroyed or removed from their positions, they simply ask for boldness to continue to advance God's Kingdom with miraculous signs and wonders.

What happens? Something I'm afraid we haven't seen enough of in our prayer meetings. The place in which they prayed is shaken, they are all filled with the Holy Spirit, and they speak the Word of God boldly. Isn't this really what we are all looking for? To me this is surgical prayer.

As we focus on the Kingdom, our attention is on establishing God's dominion through our spheres of influ-ence. How different would our prayers be if we really saw ourselves seated with Jesus right now, we are right by His side, and we're talking to Him. Imagine asking, "Lord what is it that you really want in my business? What is it that You want in this sphere where You have placed me? How do you want me to treat my employees? How do you want me to handle this or that situation?" All of a sudden His Word comes to you. "A soft answer turns away wrath, and whatever you decree shall happen."

As these words suddenly come to you, you need to realize, that's the Bible! See when the Word of God comes to you, that becomes your decree. You then begin to decree what God says. Because He is right here with us and we are seated in heavenly places, and our decree means something in the earth.

I initially learned this at the time of our building project, now in retrospect it's becoming even more revelatory to me. My closest group of advisors were predominantly carnally and naturally-minded people, which tended toward common thinking. So every time we wanted to move ahead, eight or nine people on my board basically said things like, "well we just don't have the money to do that, and prices are going up you know, remember you have to get all the building supplies from out of the country." They would frequently come to me with the problems, not the solutions. They found it hard to focus on the vision.

Focus on the Vision

So I would always have to take a position of, "I'm not going to listen to this stuff" and I'd start talking about, "I can see those pillars going up, I can see them." I'd get them on the side, and say, "Can you see all those pillars? I think there are over 2,000 pillars like this on our property. Can you see them all finished?" There they stood perplexed, just looking at huge holes in the ground!

You see, if we just kept talking about the problems, like, "We don't know how we're going to get all the cement we require, that's a lot of cement! God we need this cement. God send us the finances!" We could never accomplish the supernatural! We have to operate by faith in order to bring what all ready exists in the spirit, into reality. So I would declare in the face of this, "We have all the cement we need, it's just not on the building site yet. We have all the steel to go inside that cement, it's just not *here* yet. We have all the money we need, it's just not in the bank yet!" So what was proven to me was, as you begin to decree what you want, not what you have, as you begin to call those things that are not, as though they are, your words and prayers create the very thing you desire. Understanding this is critical to accomplishing what God has asked us to do in our domains.

Calling Those Things that are Not, As Though They Are

Now, how different would our prayer life be if we were calling those things that are not as though they were? If we just dreamed a little bit about how we see our businesses, how we see ourselves, how we see things working out for us. Yes, we may not know the specifics, but we still dream big. In my experience I didn't know the specifics, didn't know how the money was going to come. I was always surprised at where the next gift came from, and who God used to give big gifts.

I remember taking a couple of my businessmen to Spain to go and get the seating for our auditorium. Everybody thought I was crazy for wanting those chairs, but I had looked closer to home and nothing was really suitable. The chairs I had seen were fantastic; they were exactly what we needed. They were the best chairs that money could buy. There was only one catch, these were $500 chairs, $500US dollars! In fact $532US to be exact, and 3,500 of them were needed for our auditorium! Do the math! Yes! That's a lot of money. Yet that's the chair I wanted.

Well can I tell you something amazing? Four years prior to purchasing those chairs, a factory representative had come to our building site. I saw the sample he brought and decided those chairs would be wonderful. I discussed a deal with him for black chairs, because they already had an overrun on production and offered that color to me at a very reasonable price. I wanted the quality of the chair and was willing to settle for a black chair in our church if I could get that quality. Although we wanted to buy the chairs, nothing was concluded for the order. However, two years later, out of the blue we were sent a fabric sample, and were asked, if we wanted to order chairs, what color would we like. So, we looked at them and we chose a stunning blue fabric, although we already knew we could only afford the black one, and even that would stretch us, but the blue would have been perfect!

What we didn't know was that about a year and a half after the salesman had been in Zimbabwe, he was fired! The woman who took over his order book filled our order exactly to our specifications, even though we hadn't ordered the chairs. So this was the reason we landed up in Spain! The owner of the company wanted us to pay $532US per chair and had a whole factory full of our "order" of blue chairs, that we had not ordered! Now when we saw the chairs we really wanted them. So we began to discuss with the owner how we had moved from black chairs for $179US each, to blue chairs for $532US.

When we finally figured out what happened, everyone was very embarrassed. So guess what they did? They ended up selling those chairs to us for $179US each! That's still a lot of money for a chair! Now we had the chairs! But we had no money!! Now $179US when you have no money, is no different than $532US when you have no money. It really didn't matter how much the chair cost, I still had no money to pay for them. So what did we do? We began to visualize and verbalize. I had learned by now to be wise and stayed away from certain people who could only talk negatively. They talked about alternative cheap solutions which would last five years and would then need to be replaced or constantly repaired. Here we were, building a state of the art complex and I could just see how ridiculous it would be to cut corners on the chairs.

But I just kept visualizing them. So while in Spain, we cut a deal. I don't know how it all worked, it was so amazing! Because it shouldn't have worked, should it?! I mean by all banking rules it shouldn't have worked, and by all rules of negotiation it shouldn't have worked. By best business practice it shouldn't have worked. We didn't have all the money.

From Spain, I traveled to America to speak at a conference. The church I spoke at was so moved by our testimony that they gave us a $147,000 dollar offering!!!! That had never happened to our church or to their church before! I had never seen a $147,000 dollar offering, let alone received one! It was God who released that money. I knew exactly what it was for. It was for the chairs!

What was really happening is that I was seeing differently and I was decreeing differently. If I wasn't, I may have thought the money was for me to buy a Land Cruiser! I knew it was for the chairs. Not everybody saw it that way, in fact once I had the money, many thought it should be used for other parts of the building and not for chairs! Now the money from the offering was still far short of what we needed for all of the chairs, but it became the catalyst for many others in Zimbabwe to stretch their faith and begin to give towards the chairs and toward the rest of the building project.

Can you see how this thing called "faith" works? Maybe you have never caught this before, but this is faith! Now I know we've taught faith a lot in church but I'm trying to give you an essence of it. I'm trying to describe it in such a way that something opens up in your spirit. Can you get it? Can you see something?

Your Sphere of Influence

Here's what I want you to do right now. Think about your domain, the area God's given you dominion over. Now begin to picture yourself as a ruler looking at your domain from heavenly perspectives. What would your business look like if it had everything it needed. What would your domain look like if you could do anything and everything you wanted to do? If you had all the favor that you needed, if you had all the right contacts, if you had all the right equipment, if you had all the right staff and they all had the right attitudes, what would your business look like?

What would your world look like if you could decree anything and it would come to pass? Do you know what? That's EXACTLY what your business is in the spirit, and your job is to bring what you see in the spirit into reality, and you're not going to do it by saying, "O God, it's hard down here!" What you're attracting to yourself is, *it's hard*. You're attracting *hard* because that's what you're declaring, you're declaring, *it's tough, it's hard*. When you pray saying, "God I don't have enough money," you're attracting, "I don't have enough money". Whereas in reality, spiritual reality that is, you have more than enough!

So when you pray, you pray in faith, you begin to pray seeing what is done. "Father I thank you for the favor I carry in my business, I thank you that men find me, they seek me out for my counsel, for my wisdom. I thank you that I have all the equipment I need". You see, I don't know how those chairs got here, I don't know how that salesman got here, but I saw them in the spirit and I prayed, "Lord I thank you that the chairs that we need are already here." I visualized them. I see those beautiful blue chairs, I see them with deep cushions, I see them with fold up desk tops, I see them as we host conferences where 500 to 3,500 guests attend; doctors, lawyers, business professionals, church leaders using the facility and enjoying every moment because of the comfort of the seating. I began to call those things into existence. I could see that we were bringing our message of reformation by the excellence of our building and not compromising on the quality of chair.

When you pray, what you are doing is creating the picture of what you are establishing on earth. You're decreeing a thing and that's what is going to come to pass. You visualize. You begin to picture them in place. You describe them. This is the key to releasing all that God has for your sphere of dominion, your area of the Kingdom.

We have to realize that if we keep praying prayers that focus on the problems, like "poor me," "I'm a victim", "I live in Zimbabwe", "I grew up on the wrong side of the tracks", we will hinder our prayers. Don't you think God knows where we live? God has our address! God knows exactly where we're at. God knows how to get what we need to us, but we need to have faith that He can. It is important that we begin to picture what we want. What we believe God wants. If you don't know what you want, all you need to do is ask God. Scripture says, "Delight yourself in the LORD and he will give *you the desires of your heart*" (Psalm 34:7 NIV). The aim of our prayers is about establishing our Kingdom domains, our God-given spheres of influence for Him.

Are you catching this? Can you pray that way? So here's what you have to do. Whatever it takes for you to begin to visualize, just do it! Some people have to close their eyes to focus, others have to keep their eyes open. Do whatever it takes for you to begin to visualize what it is God wants. What do you want for your domain, the domain you're thinking about right now?

We've already spoken about the business domain, about how you're going to think about the business that God has for you. Though some of you are not yet business people, you do have a dream. Well, picture that dream. See it, see every detail in it. What does that business look like, and understand this, that even if it takes 25 years for that dream to come to pass the way you see it, that is what is going to happen. The way you declare it is exactly the way it is going to be. So make sure it is the dream you want and God wants, because when you start praying like this, it is magnetic. All that you are believing for starts being attracted to you and you are attracted to it.

It's important not to hinder God, because you are going to start meeting the people that are going to help you fulfill your dreams. You are going to start encountering the kind of people who will become a part of the process, because everything in the Kingdom is by relationship. Start expecting to meet the right people, to start having the right deals. Be alert and think outside the box, anything can happen. Somebody will overhear a conversation relating to an area they have been praying into. As they enquire about what they heard, "Did you say...?" The person may respond, "Yes, I said that..." "Well, you know, I know a guy you need to meet, let me introduce you." You'll just be amazed at what begins to happen. This process of seeing opportunities and net-working with relevant players, happens because you are allowing God to intervene. Angels cannot work on neg-ative prayer, they cannot bring to pass your destruction. They cannot take action on thoughts you think with a victim mentality. They only work on that which is decreed out of heaven. I know so many Christians who think they are praying, but in reality their negative speech and thoughts result in destroying themselves.

He who has ears to hear, let him hear. We need to create our pictures, whatever it takes to generate your picture, do it!

One of the most powerful weapons that God has given us for visualizing our picture is "praying in the spirit." The Bible says, "But you, beloved, building your-selves up on your most holy faith, praying in the Holy Spirit..."(Jude 1:20). When you pray in tongues, at times you start receiving a picture coming to your mind or you start getting God's Word for the moment. Often a prophesy or a word of knowledge begins to rise up from inside your heart. Don't be afraid of that prophecy, because that's going to help you decree. Write those ideas down, find time to write your dream down. Make certain it's the same dream today as it was yesterday, and make sure it's the same dream tomorrow as it was today. So once you get it, don't change dreams! One day some-body wants to be a trader, the next day they want to be a bank manager, and the next day they want to be the pres-ident of a country! Which one is it?'

What is your dream? Stop changing the dream! If you don't have a dream ask God, get God's dream for your life. Ask Him today, "show me the dream, show me my purpose." You must realize that there are stepping stones along the way. You may be doing something today that you won't be doing tomorrow, but it's equipping you for tomorrow. So don't get all hung up about it, just enjoy the journey that God is leading you on.

Nicky Ferreira

Pastor Nicky Ferreira is the pastor that heads up prayer in the church, she related the following in a testimony:

I would like to highlight both the journey and discoveries I've made whilst operating in the Prayer Domain. One of the first discoveries was on a Sunday in 1997. Pastor Tom Deuschle, our Senior Pastor of Celebration Church, had announced an urgent request to the congregation, and especially to the leaders and intercessors, to pray and fast from Monday night to Tuesday night for three specific things.

The threat of an impending cyclone, caused by the El Nino weather patterns. $15 million Zimbabwe Dollars ($1 million US at the time) for the new church building. An increase in the quality and quantity of prayer in the church.

All three of these requests were answered. The cyclone that was being caused by El Nino weakened and no longer remained a threat, finances for the building project began to noticeably increase and this target was reached within days of our prayer, although finances remained a matter of prayer throughout the building program; and yes, the level and quality of prayer began to grow. I had noticed a trend that whenever Pastor Tom declared an announcement as our spiritual oversight, the authority he carries in his office causes his pronouncements to come to pass.

It is as if the angels associated with his office are released with the speaking out of what it is God has mandated him to action. If we catch the words and agree in prayer accordingly, we see tremendous results in the church and in the lives of members of the church.

By September 1998 the numbers of people coming to our corporate, weekly, early Morning Prayer meetings had doubled. At this time, Pastor Tom released a prophetic word saying that prayer was about to be released in a new way in our church. We strongly felt at this time that we should pray daily for a week at the usual early morning Prayer time, with the prayer focusing on our Senior Pastors. At the conclusion of this week however, we were compelled by the Spirit to continue. The daily morning prayer meetings are still going strong to date. So often we had attempted to increase the amount, depth and intensity of prayer, but each time had fizzled out back to the faithful few intercessors.

Pastor Tom's prophetic word, that prompted this week of prayer, proved to be one of the keys in multiplying corporate prayer in our church. I believe the release of anointing, blessing and increase came, because we began to focus our prayers in specific areas, and to "honor" and to uphold our church's spiritual leaders.

This has created a cascade of reaction in the spirit as we see our pastors taking on new responsibilities and releasing more responsibility for prayer to us as they do. As this happens we are compelled to pray regularly for our pastor, his family and our church and the nation's leadership.

In July 2002, God opened our eyes to another key to answered prayer and blessing. A visiting pastor shared a profound word and principle with our staff at a Pastoral Leadership Meeting. He gave testimony to the wisdom and way that God had used Pastor Tom in speaking and imparting into his life. The impact of just one meeting with our *man of God* had revolutionized him and his ministry. He stated his determination and conviction to never become *too familiar* with the *man of God*. His words and testimony bore a deep witness with my own spirit and for days after this meeting I travailed in prayer for further understanding and revelation.

I knew our nation desperately needed a breakthrough and God's intervention; and my spirit also knew that we had become all *too familiar* with the "man of God" in our house. Remember, it was also said that even Jesus could do no great miracles because people saw Him only as "Joseph's son." Seeing Jesus as a mere fleshly man, diminished His divine authority and anointing to declare and manifest the Kingdom of God. I believed that our church and nation were not experiencing the breakthroughs, miracles, increase in spiritual authority, blessing, etcetera. because we, too, were not *honoring* nor expecting the right things from our "man of God", because we had allowed ourselves to commit the sin of familiarity.

I understood that unless the sin of familiarity was exposed and confessed, we would not see the power and ways of God manifested in our nation. Our Senior Pastor had been sent to this nation with an apostolic and prophetic mandate of reformation and reconciliation. I believed that God was showing us another principle and pattern that we had failed to embrace and practice. We were the cause of limiting the fullness of God and His plans, because of our corporate *sin of familiarity* and *unbelief*.

God began to confirm this because in April 2003, Pastor Tom and his wife, Pastor Bonnie were invited to Nigeria by one of the leading, apostolic church leaders in that country. When they returned, it was obvious that there was a new, increased level of anointing and authority upon their lives and ministry…our congregation could see the difference. Nigeria's Christians are noted for their strong practice of both *honoring the man of* God and supernatural giving and faith.

At the end of April 2003 the Prayer Department had planned to host its first 'Kingdom Reformation' Prayer Seminar. I had spent many hours *praying in the spirit* for this seminar, as I knew it was significant and would be used as a platform for the prayer movement we were anticipating. On the day of the scheduled seminar, when all the planning was complete and the speakers and program confirmed; God spoke to me, *"For my thoughts are not your thoughts, neither are your ways my ways…"* (Isaiah 55:8).

He used an amazing set of circumstances, unexpected encounters, conversations with people, and scriptures in our daily Bible reading all to direct me to cancel the scheduled program and, instead, dedicate the evening to *honoring* and esteeming our Senior Pastors Tom and Bonnie through words, prayers and gifts.

The evening was anything but ordinary, as God's presence and pleasure was felt by all. Something broke *in the spirit*, and also in the hearts and minds of our congregation. God was beginning to reveal His order and protocol to our church and His glorious presence and anointing were evident! We had found another key to opening a door into the *Kingdom* and *glory* of God.

Since the revelation and restoration of the principle of *honor* toward our pastors and all of those in authority *and* of *giving* of ourselves and finances has taken hold in our congregation, we have seen our pastors and church leadership operate in new levels and dimensions *in the Spirit*.

This ultimately brings *honor to God* and a greater release of His blessing and *glory*, because as we honor the gifts that he has given us and treat them with the dignity and respect they deserve, God honors us. God loves it when we respect what He respects.

Our new found love and respect for our pastors has affected every department of our church. I believe this is a vital key to the *Kingdom of God* if we want to see the revelation of Kingdom reformation, dominion and multiplication restored to the Body of Christ (Genesis 1:26-28).

In May 2002 our morning prayer meetings moved from an old office building downtown to our church's new building in the suburbs. It was a difficult and turbulent time, as many of the people who had been attending our early morning prayer meetings were now unable to attend because of the distance from work and transportation problems created by a serious fuel crisis in the country. It was also a time when two of our key prayer leaders were in transition, leaving the prayer ministry in a very vulnerable place.

By the end of 2002, I felt that the prayer ministry seemed to be dying rather than growing. I was ready to give up and cried to God to take me out of Zimbabwe for a season to refocus and renew my purpose. However, it was during this difficult time, in one of our Monday Night Prayer meetings, prophetic words began to come forth regarding a change in our prayer strategy. We were to go from being a few seasoned intercessors to becoming a strategic, praying church.

I left Zimbabwe for a much needed month holiday and break and upon my return in January 2003 I still had no clear way forward for our Prayer Department. I was called into a meeting with Pastor Tom and he presented a new *corporate prayer strategy* for our church called, *Kingdom prayer* or *domain prayer.*

It would focus on twelve domains or spheres of our society and not just our church leadership, spiritual warfare and continued repentance and intercession for the many spiritual, political and economic woes we were facing. At the core was rebuilding our nation and making prayer more practical and contagious to our larger congregation, not just the intercessors and pastors.

Our pastor was advocating practical, powerful prayer. He was giving us new keys and ideas as to how we could mobilize and multiply more people to pray intentionally and powerfully and to learn to live by conviction and biblical principle in the different domains of this nation.

This became his key pastoral, apostolic responsibility...raising up key leaders, workers, men and women to serve and minister in the different areas of society that God had called them to. His life's mission statement is *building people building dreams* and he knew if our church could promote and sustain a practical and effective prayer base it would help to rebuild and influence this nation and many other African nations.

"The kingdoms of this world have become the kingdoms of our God and of His Christ and He shall reign forever and ever..."
Revelations 11:15

God had already given our church congregation a prophetic and apostolic mandate to be a *house of prayer for all nations* (Isaiah 56:7). It was time for us to move from a growing, influential church with only a few seasoned intercessors to becoming a strategic, praying church body that was aggressively and effectively influencing all spheres of life, not just spiritually, but visibly and practically.

Pastor Tom challenged our Prayer Department and the few, faithful *intercessors* to move from praying in small, but intense Morning Prayer groups, to praying daily in a bigger and broader prayer format. He encouraged us to use the "Lord's Prayer" as a template, worshipping and exalting His name, praying for heaven to be revealed on earth, and then praying specifically and practically for the twelve domains (spheres of society) that he had identified. This was all a part of the "new beginnings and new things" that had been prophesied earlier and it was now time to implement. Although Zimbabwe was being dominated by a *spirit of lawlessness and witchcraft*, God was going to give us an increase and authority in prayer and keys to the *mystery of His Kingdom*. We were about to see God move in ways we couldn't imagine.

As God challenged our congregation to touch heaven and His heart through worship, praise and prayer, we felt compelled to mobilize increasing numbers of church members to take the *Kingdom* to the marketplace, and not limit our message to within our church walls or small-thinking.

For by him all things were created: things in heaven and on earth, visible and invisible, whether thrones or powers or rulers or authorities; all things were created by him and for him.

...so that in everything he might have the supremacy.
Colossians 1:16,18 (NIV)

In early 2003, Pastor Tom called the prayer department, along with some of our church's key players in the business community, education field, a few of our Christian doctors, members working in government and also some Christian men who were leaders in the advertisement, printing and marketing industry, to help him launch the *Kingdom Prayer* strategy. His goal was to identify, recruit and raise up an effective team of committed Prayer Leaders for each of the twelve domains, to mobilize and motivate them to participate in this new strategy for prayer and nation-building. They would focus on their domain's interests and passions and take responsibility to use their individual influence to recruit other Christians to join in domain prayer, this we felt could become a powerful movement.

The goal was to enlarge our growing church's dwindling prayer base by organizing corporate prayer meetings that were practical, powerful and family-friendly. If we didn't start praying corporately, changing our thinking and doing something different and drastic soon, Zimbabwe and most of Sub-Sahara Africa were destined to continue in a rapid decline. God was reminding us that His words to Adam in the garden were still His original mandate for discipleship and advancing the *Kingdom of God* (*Genesis 1:26-28*). We must focus our prayers and purpose in subduing and influencing everything that God created.

In early April 2003 our church hosted a *Kingdom Reformation* prayer launch week and invited the newly identified prayer leaders and those they had invited from each of the twelve domains, to catch the vision and fire for corporate prayer. The week proved more than a success, and a year later we had between 70-150 people from different spheres every morning attending a corporate prayer meeting that focuses on praying for the twelve domains and key issues facing each. This Kingdom reformation prayer is now helping to disciple a nation! The results continue to amaze us."

PART TWO

Principles for Transformation

"Prayer does not stand alone. It is not an isolated duty and independent principle. It lives in association with other Christian duties, it is wedded to other principles, is a partner with other graces."

E.M. Bounds

Chapter 3
Surgical Prayer is Precise

Having discovered God's mandate for us to start employing surgical prayer and having clarified what we mean by our domains or our spheres of influence, we then started to develop the process of "how to" pray surgically. God always works with patterns and principles, and as we began to apply one part of surgical prayer the rest of these patterns and principals emerged.

Almost immediately we discovered that surgical prayer entails praying with precision and accuracy. The more we can target our prayers, the more powerful our prayers are likely to be.

All Manner of Prayer

God will answer all our prayers. God wants every single prayer that we pray to be answered. If our prayers are not being answered however, could it be that we are missing something? When the body of Christ learns how to pray effectively we can change any circumstance. We can have victory where there has been defeat, we can have healing where there has been sickness, we can have life where there has been death. When we pray in accordance with God's Word we are going to see God's results, we are going to see victory.

We are instructed to pray with all manner of prayer.

Pray at all times (on every occasion, in every season) in the Spirit, with all [manner of] prayer and entreaty.

Ephesians 6:18 (AMP)

When I came to Africa, the sporting disciplines that I was used to in the United States were for the most part, foreign to this part of the world. I'll never forget going to my first rugby game, and trying to understand the game with American football rules in my mind, and then on to cricket, trying to understand it with baseball rules in my mind. My only conclusion was that these people had no idea how to play the game. I soon realized that the problem was not the game but my understanding of the rules that governed the game. So it is in the realm of corporate prayer. When God says to, "pray with all manner of prayer" it simply means there are different rules for different manner of prayer. Just as cricket being played with baseball rules would lead to a lack of precision, purpose, and continuity in the game and result in chaos, so corporate and individual prayer each operate differently. Although similar, the rules of one are not directly applicable to the other. The impact on the players or participants, is the same, a lack of interest, lack of understanding and little effectiveness.

Unity of Purpose

So it is with corporate prayer, not only do we all have to be playing the same game and with the same rules, but we must also understand the power of "unity of purpose" and "unity of mind." As I have led corporate prayer, and attended literally thousands of prayer meetings I have noticed that very often the lack of unity and the lack of focus keeps us from precision in our prayers. A team is only as strong as its focus. In corporate prayer we are only as strong as our ability to focus together in agreement.

I often think of my childhood years playing baseball. It always seemed that there were one or two kids that just didn't get what the game was all about. So, when it came time to positioning people in the field, inevitably, we would take our absent-minded friends and put them in right field where the least activity took place and where they could do the least damage to the team. I can recall on at least two occasions in my little league career where our right fielder was chasing butterflies or picking dandelions, or some other equally unfocused activity when the game-winning ball was hit in their direction. Needless to say, that player would feel terrible after the game, but when we asked him what he was doing, for the life of him he couldn't tell us, but as our coach would tell us later, "His head just wasn't in the game!" So it is with prayer. Often either our heads are not in the game or we are focused on our own immediate concerns.

Some of the causes of absent-minded praying are; lack of knowledge about what is being prayed about, lack of understanding of how to pray, or undisciplined habits that have been left unchecked in corporate prayer.

Pray with Understanding

One of the greatest distractions to effective praying in corporate prayer meetings is when people only pray in tongues. A topic is raised, we all agree it needs to be prayed about, and then everyone rattles off in tongues for the next period of time, until the next topic is raised. The problem with this is that often the person's mind is totally disengaged. I've often felt like tapping someone who is praying in tongues on the shoulder, and asking, "do you have any idea what we're praying about?" The apostle Paul exhorts us,

"I will pray in the spirit and I will pray in my understanding." Focusing our attention on what the spirit is focused on, will help us increase our precision in prayer. When we lose focus and become distracted, no amount of speaking in tongues will help us to focus. It is imperative that we develop the skill of articulating in our understanding what God is directing us to pray for.

Paul said, concerning corporate meetings in First Corinthians 14:18,19 (NKJV):

I thank my God I speak with tongues more than you all;

yet in the church I would rather speak five words with my understanding, that I may teach others also, than ten thousand words in a tongue.

Understanding Versus Trust

The second greatest hindrance to precision is on the opposite end of the spectrum and has to do with becoming so focused on knowing and understanding everything before praying, that we hinder our ability to pray beyond what we can comprehend. There are two kinds of knowledge, one is revelation knowledge and the other stems from an inquisitive mind. When it comes to precision in prayer an overactive mind can be a hindrance. The Bible teaches that spiritual things are spiritually understood.

This is what we speak, not in words taught us by human wisdom but in words taught by the Spirit, expressing spiritual truths in spiritual words.

The man without the Spirit does not accept the things that come from the Spirit of God, for they are foolishness to him, and he cannot understand them, because they are spiritually discerned.

1 Corinthians 2:13,14 (NIV)

For this reason we also, from the day we heard of it, have not ceased to pray and make [special] request for you, [asking] that you may be filled with the full (deep and clear) knowledge of his will in all spiritual wisdom [in comprehensive insight into the ways and purposes of God] and in understanding and discernment of spiritual things.
Colossians 1:9 (AMP)

When we pray it is natural for us to try and understand "how" our prayer will be answered. This often leads the active mind into a subtle trap, whose end result leads to unbelief and unanswered prayer. If you must know "how" your prayer will be answered before you pray, that is not faith, but is the work of the flesh. When the mind has to put our answers in the context of what can be perceived by our physical senses, then the net result is that our spirits become subject to our minds and our flesh. Prayers of faith are declarations and actions based on obedience to spiritual patterns and principles. Ours is to know "what" to pray, not to know "how" our prayer will be answered.

Kingdom prayers are like a man who sows seed in a field and does not know if it will spring up or produce a crop, but trusts that as he continues to water the seed, he will reap a harvest.

He also said, "This is what the kingdom of God is like. A man scatters seed on the ground.

Night and day, whether he sleeps or gets up, the seed sprouts and grows, though he does not know how.

All by itself the soil produces grain—first the stalk, then the head, then the full kernel in the head.

As soon as the grain is ripe, he puts the sickle to it, because the harvest has come."
Mark 4:26-29 (NIV)

This lesson of obedience and faith, and of not trusting or leaning on our own understanding, is one of the greatest challenges to answered prayer. I have had the privilege of knowing many farmers in my life. They all have amazing faith to go and borrow money, purchase seed, plant their seed and then expect a harvest that will pay back their loans and have enough to supply all of their other needs. But one thing I know is that every farmer I have ever met is focused on one thing during the farming season, making sure that the crop has every chance to produce a harvest. For the most part this entails watering and weeding the field. I've never seen a farmer uncover his seed to determine if his crop is growing or not. Instead he had absolute faith that what he has planted will produce even though he doesn't understand how it does so.

In 2 Kings 5:10-12, we see the story of Naaman the leper, commander of the army of the king of Syria, responding to a servant girl's testimony of the greatness of her God. The story played out to the point where he eventually stands before Elisha's servant and is simply told to bathe seven times in the Jordan River so that, "his flesh would be restored and he would be made clean." But Naaman became angry and had preconceived ideas of what the prophet should do, "behold I thought he would surely come out to me, and stand, and call on the name of the Lord his God, and wave his hand over the place, and heal the leper." Then his mind took him even further, "are not Abana and Pharpar, rivers of Damascus better than all the waters of Israel? May I not wash in them and be clean? So he turned away and went away in a rage."

I encounter this kind of thinking often with Christians who know *what* they want before they pray, but also want to prescribe *how*, *why*, *when* and *where* the answer is going to occur. Eventually when Naaman simply obeyed, the Bible says, "his flesh was restored like that of a little child, and he was clean."

I am convinced that accurate, piercing prayer will change nations. Accurate, piercing prayer will change our families, will change our financial situations, and will bring healing. When we learn how to pray accurately and state the specifics by faith, and we act as though the principles and patterns of the Word of God are reliable and true, and when we can accurately see the answer as we pray, then God is able to respond to us and we will recognize when he does.

For the Word of God is living and powerful and sharper than any two-edged sword, piercing even to the dividing apart of soul and spirit, and of the joints and marrow, it is a discerner of the thoughts and intents of the heart.
Hebrews 4:12 (NKJV)

The wording used here is only used in this passage of Scripture and the idea in the Greek language is of a surgeon who uses his scalpel to dissect between the joints and the marrow of the bone. Now that is sharp, piercing and accurate. This is the kind of prayer that the Word of God directs us into. Similarly, Isaiah 49:2 says, God is intent on using sharp instruments in prayer. His Word, and His Word in our mouths, are some of the most important weapons in our arsenal.

God answers prayer on the basis of what people ask Him, as illustrated in the story of the blind men in Matthew 20:29-34. Their crying out to Jesus for *pity* and *mercy* were vague prayers. The blind men did not specify exactly what they wanted. Once Jesus got them to ask specifically for what they wanted, He was able to act immediately and gave them what they asked for. The idea of specificity is critical to piercing prayer.

Part of our vision is, *transforming lives, reforming nations*. Only the light of a reformation message can pierce the darkness that shrouds people's minds. Dr Myles Munroe in his book, *Rediscovering the Kingdom* said, "The goal of communication is to transfer the ideas in your mind to another mind."

But even if our gospel is veiled, it is veiled to those who are perishing,

whose minds the god of this age has blinded who do not believe, lest the light of the gospel of the glory of Christ, who is the image of God, should shine on them.

2 Corinthians 4:3,4 (NKJV)

In the beginning was the Word, and the Word was with God, and the Word was God.

He was in the beginning with God.

All things were made through him, without him nothing was made that was made.

In him was life, and that life was the light of men.

And the light shines in the darkness, and the darkness did not comprehend it.

John 1:1-5 (NKJV)

Testimony: Jakes Chiduku

The story of Jakes Chiduku, and his wife and family, whose lives have truly been radically transformed as they have applied the Kingdom principles, is nothing less than remarkable. The following is his testimony.

Sometime in November 2005 just before the onset of the rains, the Mazowe River, which is the main source for irrigation water to our farm, had run dry and on top of that, was soon overrun by gold panners, causing degradation and destruction of the riverbed.

Our main water source for the season was completely destroyed and I had lost hope in the coming season.

I made up my mind that I would only do a small hectarage, which was to be irrigated by borehole water. After seeking God about the cropping programme, the Lord led me to a Scripture and through the verse I read, I believe He clearly told me that "He who watches the wind will not sow and he who observes the clouds will not reap" (Ecclesiastes 11:4 NIV). So, after this word, I planted on dry ground, which is not the normal agricultural practice. The same night I went outside with my three children and after a short talk, I asked them to pray for a good rainy season.

We all went to sleep and about two hours later it began to rain cats and dogs. For us that was the beginning of what we now call "the season".

Later when the crop had emerged, my wife and I frequently walked in the lands confessing and affirming that we would see a harvest of 3,45 tonnes (7590 pounds) per hectare (2.5 acres). At first I was conservative because my highest yield to date had only been 1,2 tones per hectare (2.5 acres). My wife Lily was bold, and I was nervous to hear her 3,45 tones/hectare confession, but as time went on, I later joined in her confession and at harvest we actually realized an average of four tonnes per hectare for the very first time in our farming career. In the farming sector this is considered an extremely good yield. My wife and I have now set this as our minimum target.

The picture of our lives was not always so positive, in fact before we found ourselves joined to Celebration Church, our life and our prospects for the future was bleak to say the least. Let me just give an account of our journey:

November 1998 we moved to Celebration Ministries. We were going through a very difficult time in our life, financially, socially and spiritually and our marriage was on the rocks.

I was unemployed and unable to pay our bills so our electricity supply was off more than it was on and we also were struggling to pay our children's school fees. We survived by going to fields and picking weeds like nyeve (a kind of wild spinach), bonongwe (pigweed) to eat, and then even resorted to picking up a dead rabbit by the roadside just so we could see ourselves through another day. We convinced our son that the homemade lemonade from the tree in our yard was really special to take as a drink at school.

We sold empty bottles from our garage, and even looked for them as we walked the street, just so we could buy a bit of Kapenta fish (a fresh water sardine, known in the vernacular as matemba) for our meals.

My last job was in the informal sector at Mbare Msika, the local market, where I sold commercial maize in buckets just like a vegetable vendor.

This business never got very far, as the margins were too small and the price of maize was regulated, so I became a full time house-husband with nothing to do except fetch and carry children.

I was handed over to the lawyers and debt collectors. Twice the messenger of court came to attach my property. As a last resort I used my wife's car (a 2-door coupe) as a "pirate taxi" (unlicensed and illegal transport) to afford money for bread.

In 2002, I was falsely accused for theft and got incarcerated but was later acquitted and set free.

All I could see was my life spiraling out of control and in a downward direction.

When I joined the church I was at first not sure whether I had joined the right one or not, as most of the people seemed very prosperous, and it seemed all of the cars in the parking lot were of a very late model. I felt very intimidated and out of place. However, I decided to get involved in church activities and served as part of the welcome team, first time counseling and got involved on the building site of the church's new sanctuary. The events which have taken place in my life and that of my wife and family as a result of getting involved at Celebration Church, and following the Kingdom principles laid out so clearly by Pastor Tom are so numerous and amazing that I have listed them so that others can see the hand of God in my life and give Him glory.

Nine months after joining Celebration Church I was able to negotiate a six year lease on a farm. I applied for funding from every bank in the country but I was turned down.

I persuaded my wife Lily to leave her job and she got a package of $137,000 which we used to buy soy bean seed.

We moved to the farm by faith without any funding. All we had was our furniture. We trusted God to meet our needs and provide our inputs.

God provided what we came to know as 'vision helpers', they arrived almost miraculously as we needed them. Some of them came with expert guidance, and there were others who came with tractors and equipment to help plant a crop for us.

I am so grateful to God, who has now raised us from sitting behind a bucket of maize at Mbare, and today, I now sit on three major agricultural related company boards as a director. From being self-employed, I now employ more than 200 people.

I came to the farm with just my furniture, but I now have enough equipment to do all my farming operation.

From struggling with ZESA (Zimbabwe Electricity Supply Authority) bills I now have my own generator capable of supplying power for my use and that of my employees.

Within two years of starting my operation, by the grace of God, I had paid all my debts and bought my own farming equipment and was now on a cash basis. As I look back, I am now glad that I was not funded by the bank as the interest rates went through the roof.

From struggling to pay my son's school fees I'm now paying my children's school fees as well as those of 31 orphaned children.

From selling maize in buckets at Mbare Musika, I now produce foundation A and B seed maize.

From pirating in a 2-door sports car for a morsel of bread, I now produce the wheat that makes the bread and God has blessed me with a land cruiser VX 100 series while my wife drives a C class 200 Kompressor Mercedes Benz. In all we have seven cars.

To cap it all, I have enrolled with an aviation school for private pilot license and that should tell you our next move.

God has blessed me and caused me to be a blessing to many. I didn't know the principles that I live by today, until Pastor Tom then delivered to us and set us free from the laws of sin and death. I am eternally grateful to see the principles of God's Kingdom working in my life, and the power of specific targeted prayer availing on behalf of me and my family. I thank God in my every remembrance of Pastor Tom, and pay tribute to Pastor Tom, to Pastor Bonnie and to their family for their faithfulness to persevere in the vision and mission God has given them for us and for the world, of Building People, Building Dreams. These truths are "life to us who have found them and health to our whole body" (Proverbs 4:22 NIV).

Chapter 4
Surgical Prayer is Penetrating

In the last chapter we said that surgical prayer is precise, this has to do with accuracy. The next aspect of surgical prayer is that it is penetrating, which is the ability to be both accurate, and forceful as well as to saturate and permeate. It is the ability to breakthrough and into.

The word *penetrate* is derived from the Latin word, *penetro*, "a point, meaning, to enter; to pass into the interior; as, to penetrate a country. It also means to work behind enemy lines, breakthrough enemy lines, penetrate into enemy territory."

In our world's most recent wars within the first few weeks of attacking Afghanistan or Iraq the Allied forces held air supremacy, which meant that no enemy aircraft were able to fly in any airspace over the country. In order to have air supremacy not only did the opposing air force have to be grounded, but the Allied Forces had to knock out the enemy's radar and their ability to communicate.

Once this was accomplished deploying ground troops was far less risky, allowing rapid penetration into the enemy territory. Extrapolating this you can see the powerful and vast meaning of *penetration*. It includes capturing control and influence over areas from which dominion can be exercised.

Bunker-Buster Prayers

In the opening chapter, I wrote about smart bombs which are known for their accuracy, as opposed to carpet bombs. As Allied Forces were confronted with underground bunkers that were seemingly impenetrable by most smart bombs and carpet bombing, they invented a 908 kg smart bomb, that could be guided with pinpoint accuracy, and penetrate these seemingly impenetrable areas. These bombs were commonly referred to as "bunker-busters".

We often think of prayer as simply a breakthrough, or piercing through the shell of resistance. It is far more than just a breakthrough that is needed, rather a penetration, which is best accomplished as we harness numbers of people and pray corporately. This is not to minimize the prayers of the individual, however corporate prayer produces an increased thrust. Where there is collective evil, its powers cannot be broken by individual intercessors, nor by silent prayer walks or spiritual mapping. All of these are incomplete processes unless they are matched with corporate, united, focused prayer.

If we will continue to press together in the same direction, we can actually achieve an advance. I've often given the illustration of the futility of someone punching in different directions at the same time, in doing so you couldn't punch your way out of a wet paper bag, because you are dissipating your strength by striking in divergent directions, but as you focus all your punches in one direction, the collective impact produces a breakthrough. You can push your way out of something, a solid thrust in one direction can result in a break out.

It is one thing to pierce, but it's quite another thing to penetrate. Just because enemy lines have been broken into does not mean that territory has been taken. Penetrating prayer results in *taking territory*, and includes both strategy and perseverance.

Leaders or Lone Rangers

A part of this Kingdom strategy is understanding the role leaders play in accomplishing penetration and perseverance. God appoints and uses leaders to direct His breakthroughs. He gives His strategy to His apostles and prophets, and it's up to the Church to follow the given strategy. The Children of Israel needed God and a leader, Joshua, to actually take the land that had been given them by God. This took a long time, required obedience to God's strategy given through His leaders, which in turn required trust in the leader, self-sacrifice to follow rather than stay comfortable, and perseverance on the part of the Israelites for the battles that followed. We all have leaders God intends for us to follow. It's easy to follow a leader when the going is good. The hard part for both leaders and followers is to both lead and follow when the going is tough. Hard as it was, Israel had to follow Joshua's instructions in order to succeed in taking and keeping the promised land.

Just as God had given the promised land to the Israelites, "it is your Father's good pleasure to give us the Kingdom" (Luke 12:32)!

The similarities to us now are noteworthy. We tend to have the perception that ownership of spiritual domains for the Kingdom means it has been handed to us on a platter or sent through the mail. This is not so, the reality is that action and effort is required to secure ownership of anything anywhere. With the Kingdom of God, we must align ourselves with God's revealed principles of how ownership and possession works. We understand it belongs to us, it is our entitlement, but the current reality is that it is occupied, as it was for the Israelites. Jesus has overcome the powers of darkness, but we have to go up and take dominion of this spiritual territory. This is Kingdom thinking about ownership, and is in line with the children of God coming into their own.

> **For the earnest expectation of the creation eagerly waits for the revealing of the sons of God.**
>
> **Romans 8:19 (NKJV)**

Just as it took tough battles and perseverance for the Israelites to go in and take the promised land, it will take determination and faith for the children of God to exercise their covenant rights now and take dominion of the territories God has allotted to us. Although "The earth is the LORD's, and everything in it, the world, and all who live in it" (Psalm 24:1 NIV), it does not become a reality in our lives until we then occupy it, utilize it, inhabit and cultivate it.

In the New Testament we see that everywhere Paul went, he penetrated the culture of the city or country he preached in. He did this not by spending hours prayer walking or spiritual mapping, but as he boldly preached and prayed, with accompanying signs and wonders, which brought him face to face with the powers of darkness. Paul constantly received instruction from the Holy Spirit, and exerted extreme determination and energy to accomplish this, and experienced conflict in the process.

> **experiencing the same conflict which you saw in me, and now hear is in me.**
>
> **Philippians 1:30 (NASB)**

> **For I want you to know what a great conflict I have for you and those in Laodicea, and for as many a have not seen my face in the flesh.**
>
> **Colossians 2:1 (NKJV)**

This was all part of penetration of the territory or domain he was given to take possession of. Paul was exercising control and influence in the spiritual realm in his domain as an apostle in specified regions, and as he did so there was a resultant surge in demonic reaction. It's been said that Nero's persecution was hell's response to Paul's preaching! Whether that was the case or not, the fact is that Paul effectively penetrated the region of Asia Minor for the Kingdom of God, and the effects are still being felt today. His life and ministry brought about an expansion of the Kingdom of God, that was as significant as it was defining.

The Power of Perseverance

The principle of perseverance is central to penetration. A once-off prayer meeting is unlikely to accomplish much in dealing with centuries-old national problems. Daniel had to push through for 21 days in order to receive the answer to his prayer and achieve a much needed penetration. One of our key statements is, "Perseverance outlasts persecution." We have learned that this attribute is critical to effective prayer that will penetrate.

As previously stated, "God had given me a mandate to build a church, a family of believers, that would bring about transformation and reformation in Africa and affect the world, starting in Zimbabwe." As stated earlier, the aim of the Gospel of the Kingdom is to replicate heaven on earth, and God's rulership in the lives of His people. Jesus Himself taught His disciples to pray, "*Your*

Kingdom come, *Your* will be done on earth as it is in heaven" (Matthew 6:10 NKJV).

This Kingdom Gospel therefore should produce evidence to all nations, *that* God sent Jesus' (John 17:21). The Lord Jesus says, "This Gospel of the Kingdom shall be preached in the whole world as a testimony to all the nations, and then the end will come" (Matthew 24:14). *Kerusso* is the word here translated as *preach*, which means to publish or proclaim, and *testimony* here is the word *marturion*, meaning something *evidential*, or *evidence* given. In other words it is factual verification or proof of something.

The pertinent question to consider at this point is, has the church to date, persevered in application of the Word, to produce evidence of the rule of God, that can be broadcast to all nations and accurately convey who God is. Certainly the Church has made headlines for ungodly behavior, but few headlines with proof of His governance. Jesus clearly tells us what evidence will convince the world:

> **By this all will know that you are My disciples, if you have love for one another.** John 13:35 (NKJV)

In His last recorded prayer before the crucifixion Jesus gives a second characteristic that we should exhibit as proof to the world of who we are.

> **...that they also may be one in Us, so that the world may believe that You sent Me.** John 17:21b (NASB)

Corporate revelation is necessary for corporate practice of the Kingdom! I realized that we as a church therefore, must have this understanding ourselves, and learn to apply this revelation in our own personal, family and church lives, before we can take this to the nation and the world. We have to live this *Kingdom life* here in Zimbabwe first.

Practical application of this *Kingdom life* can prove to be challenging. It's obvious that for anything to occur corporately, everyone must be united in intent. Frequently however people's feelings *run high* if their personal space is infringed upon. Many of us have grown up with a basic core value of personal freedom, and in fact believe that Christianity supports that view, the world today espouses a Christianity which is *just me and God*, a relationship with a personal Saviour. We all understand that a kingdom is an area in which a king rules and people are subject to that king, not only individually, but corporately.

So, to live a Kingdom lifestyle means submission to a king, thinking and living with others according to Kingdom values, and having a vision to extend the Kingdom. The aim of persevering, bunker-busting prayer, is to extend the Kingdom of God in our domain, both individually and corporately.

The Zimbabwe Picture

Back to our application in Zimbabwe. The picture in Zimbabwe was not looking good! Over the past 25 years there had been numerous attempts at finding methods to answer the issues in the nation of Zimbabwe. Many of these were centered around prayer. At the onset there were many major ministries coming into the country and leading churches, individuals and intercessors to what they considered to be spiritual high places. The thought behind this was to cast down every demonic spirit and break their influence over the nation. Prayer mapping conferences lasting weeks sent people scurrying throughout the city to identify every brothel, bar, Masonic lodge, cult and witches coven, etcetera in the city. Select groups went on prayer walks and secret excursions into cemeteries and national monuments, where oil and communion elements were used to supposedly purify the land. My observations are that many of those who involved themselves in these practices became disillusioned and eventually were spiritually shipwrecked. They focused more on the power of the enemy, than on the power of God, and although they spent a great deal of time trying to dismantle the enemy's power, the fruit of answered prayer is sorely lacking in the scope of a 25 year history of praying this type of prayer.

During this time we saw the nation progressively deteriorate throughout most sectors of society; most notably economically, but also in the health sector, in education, in farming, in banking and in business.

Prophecies proliferated, declaring turn-around times for the nation or the demise of the current leadership. These prophecies were often punctuated with set times, anything from six months all the way to six years. Unfortunately the years continued to roll by and the situation continued to deteriorate in the eyes of most prayer leaders and pastors.

My observation is that it is not our responsibility to go looking for enemies or to move onto enemy territory. But as we advance God's Kingdom and penetrate the various domains that He gives us, with the aim of establishing ourselves in these domains, plenty of opportunities arise to deal with the opposition at hand. Choosing to chase the demonic strongholds became a distraction to establishing Kingdom practice and rule in individual lives, families, churches and businesses. I had taught, "You become what you behold." Our mental and emotional awareness is impacted by what our senses are assimilating, which directly affects our thoughts and behavior.

Binding and Loosing

With our mandate, to effectively and measurably bring about positive Kingdom changes beginning in Zimbabwe, I realized there had to be something in all of these teachings although I felt like there was something missing, at least in regard to emphasis. If, in fact we were to have dominion on earth, there would need to be some control over "the heavenlies" as many of the prophetic and intercessory teachers were wrestling with.

Part of this answer lay in the all too familiar Scripture:

> **Assuredly, I say to you, whatever you bind on earth will be bound in heaven, and whatever you loose on earth will be loosed in heaven.**
>
> **Again I say to you that if two of you agree on earth concerning anything that they ask, it will be done for them by My Father in heaven.**
>
> **For where two or three are gathered together in My name, I am there in the midst of them.**
>
> **Matthew 18:18-20 (NKJV)**

We had spent a great deal of time on the *binding* aspect of this scripture to the neglect of the *loosing*, and our emphasis had seemed to shift from binding things on earth to binding things in the heavenlies. I became aware of a need to begin to focus on loosing things on earth by faith. The atmosphere in Zimbabwe during the 25 years since independence filled people's conversations with complaints and criticisms, fear and anxiety. Even in the church very few were speaking "Thy Kingdom come, Thy will be done on earth as it is in heaven." I realized that the key to penetration was the way we speak and pray. If we changed the way we spoke and prayed, both individually and corporately, we would begin to see Kingdom rule established. "The creative power is in the tongue, God spoke and it was! We needed to start creating our environment through the power of our declarations. God has already modeled what we are to do, and we just needed to follow suit."[1]

As Paul says in Colossians 1:16 (NKJV):

For by Him all things were created that are in heaven and that are on earth, visible and invisible, whether thrones or dominions or principalities or powers. All things were created through Him and for Him.

So as we apply Kingdom speaking and prayer personally as well as corporately, we will see Kingdom rule established in our lives. Only then can we move from a position of strength to bring about transformation and reformation in the areas we have influence over. We can only lead where we have been, and influence what we ourselves have experienced.

Spiritual Protocol

This change takes place according to a pattern which God gives and is laid forth in Deuteronomy, where God tells the children of Israel how He's going to let them conquer the land, little by little, according to their strength.

The LORD your God will drive out those nations before you, little by little. You will not be allowed to eliminate them all at once, or the wild animals will multiply around you.   **Deuteronomy 7:22 (NIV)**

It has been foolishness for us to think that through spiritual warfare we will be able to deal with huge demonic spiritual principalities on our own, or at our own behest. There seems to be almost a sense of fantasy

---

1 *The Creative Power of the Tongue* by Charles Capps

in many people's prayers. If we pray violently enough, or long enough, or in a certain location, our prayers will be heard, or will at least be more effective. This is contrary to Biblical teaching. God has set lines of authority, which even the Lord Jesus is submitted to. "No one knows about that *day or hour*, not even the angels in heaven, nor the Son, but only the Father." When Daniel was interceding, the response to his prayer that was delivered by the angel Gabriel was, "the prince of the Persian kingdom resisted me twenty-one days. Then Michael, one of the chief princes, came to help me, because I was detained there with the king of Persia" (Daniel 10:13). Again Michael instructs Daniel saying, "Do you know why I have come to you? Soon I will return to fight against the prince of Persia, and when I go, the prince of Greece will come" (Daniel 10:20). In both of these cases it is very clear who is doing the fighting. God is not irresponsible, He is not going to use a novice to confront a principality. Princes address princes, kings address kings. Daniel prayed, but the angels did the fighting.

Daniel understood spiritual protocol and doctrine. In order for us to succeed in breakthrough we also need this understanding. Hearing instruction from our spiritual leadership and following that is a part of this protocol. Earlier in this chapter, I detailed that one critical aim of an army is to "knock out the enemy's radar and their ability to communicate…thus allowing rapid penetration into the enemy territory." This applies not only to the enemy, but to our own communication. Ambiguous or incorrect intercommunication, whether deliberate or unintentional can be lethal in a war. These principles apply to our situation, where we are in a spiritual battle, placed under spiritual authority by God. We need to be careful to receive instructions correctly as well as relay them clearly, cognizant that, whether intentionally or accidentally, communications that are indistinct or obscure result in confusion. Again scripture instructs us, "a kingdom divided against itself will fall" (Luke 10:17).

So what may confuse our communications? A primary cause is when the sheep have a different vision from the shepherd, an army a different aim to their commander, a team a different play to their coach. A different vision is di-vision. This presents an unwillingness to hear instruction, direction and strategy.

The eye is the lamp of the body. If your eyes are good, your whole body will be full of light.

But if your eyes are bad, your whole body will be full of darkness. If then the light that is in you is darkness, how great is the darkness! Matthew 6:22,23 (NIV)

So what might make the eye bad, what might block our vision?

For all that is in the world, the lust of the flesh and the lust of the eyes and the boastful pride of life, is not from the Father, but is from the world.

1 John 2:16 (NASB)

Translated, that means anything that takes our attention and affection away from God or hinders our communication with each other is lethal to us, we no longer walk in the light, nor therefore in the Kingdom. One of the greatest obstructions to clear spiritual vision currently in modern society is a form of idolatry deeply embedded inside our economic systems. If we are going to have real reformation, it will be in the face of an ever-increasing fascination with materialism. The apostle Paul warned of a time when people would think that godliness would be associated with great gain personally. This is not untrue but is only half of the picture. God is very interested in prospering His people, not only for their own blessing but primarily with the view in mind of extending His Kingdom. I believe the reason that Islam is so powerful is because its followers have made it a way of life. Islam is shaking conventional economic systems. Because of targeted use of finances the power of Islam is putting pressure on institutions once clearly influenced by Christian values.

As many Christians pursue personal wealth there's an unwillingness to risk life, honor or fortune for the Kingdom of God. The shocking fact is that by exalting wealth, life, honor and fortune, subtly they become the idols of choice, both blocking our clarity of vision, as well as locking us into a lifeless form of religion, "denying the power thereof" (2 Timothy 3:5). A significant part of being reformers is demonstrated by our willingness to use our finances to accurately impact the areas and domains we are praying about. Putting "our money where our mouths are."

Part of being reformers is the willingness to use our finances sacrificially to impact the areas and domains we are praying about.

A definitive aspect of the growth of our prayer meetings is the amount of finances sown into the things that we are praying about. This has become a hallmark of our prayer meetings, in as much as our prayer department is one of the most well-funded departments in the church. Those who come to pray realize that, "they cannot appear before God empty-handed" (Exodus 23:15, 34:20, Deuteronomy 16:16). Until the level of sacrifice that we are willing to operate at, exceeds the amount of sacrifice which our contemporaries are giving to ancestral spirits through spirit mediums and other witchcraft practices, we will not see the Kingdom established.

Examples have begun to start pouring in of how sacrifice breaks the power of darkness over our lives. Mostly these are still at an individual level. I have given a couple of these examples here, to show you the extremely practical application of the power of the Word of God on sacrifice today. This must, and I believe will, grow to be corporate and on to national and international levels of testimony.

Testimony: Claudia Muvuti

The first report is from Sister Claudia Muvuti, who has been under my teachings on the power of sacrifice and has received life-changing revelation of its authority in the spiritual realm. Her testimony demonstrates the magnitude of the power of sacrifice in a situation of great gravity. Hear her story:

"In 2006 my husband and I had experienced some problems in our marriage and did not know why. During one particularly powerful ladies meeting, Pastor Bonnie had a guest speaker sharing her testimony on marriage. Whilst she was sharing, the Holy Spirit told me to sacrifice my wedding ring. I battled with this because it not only had great monetary value, but also great sentimental value. I eventually obeyed. When I put the ring on the Pastor's hand, she almost fell backwards because she said the Lord had showed her the ring before the service. I didn't understand why the Holy Spirit asked me to sacrifice the ring.

The Holy Spirit showed me weeks later that my husband's parents had been divorced after seven years of marriage. In his first marriage my husband himself had also been divorced after seven years of marriage and this was our seventh year of marriage! The sacrifice broke the cycle and the power of divorce and we have now been married for ten years. Through this I discovered the power of obedience and sacrifice. My marriage today is a result of Pastor

Tom and Pastor Bonnie's obedience to the call to this nation, Zimbabwe, and the nations of the world.

The second testimony is from brothers George and Cliff Chitsinde. Listen as they share their story.

Testimony: George and Cliff Chitsinde

Our family has been heavily steeped in ancestral worship for generations; one of our aunts (tete) is a spirit medium. We grew up knowing that she is filled with fearful spirits and she was to be consulted on all major family decisions. Upon her instructions the family travelled all over the country to the different shrines to perform ritual upon ritual. Whatever instruction she gave, these were obediently followed by all. We all lived in fear of her and what possessed her, but this was all the family knew, as far back as my grandfather's generation.

The family spent a lot of money on maintaining this way of life — we used to buy the animals that were slaughtered for sacrifices; we would buy all the apparel that she would wear for rituals. At one point we made a major financial sacrifice and went to the Department of Natural Museums and Monuments to buy elephant's feet made into stools. These were very expensive but were deemed a worthy gift to the high gods. We revered these gods. We were in such awe of them that anything the spirit-medium said they needed we would diligently find.

At one point the two of us started a small corporation that became extremely prosperous and we were under instruction to take a portion of the profits and put them on a special plate that she had given us. This money was used by the spirit-medium, but as time went on things started going wrong in the company and we started losing money despite these monthly sacrifices. What was interesting about this is that our grandfather used to tell us stories about how wealthy he had been as a young man, but now we saw an old man with absolutely nothing to his name. The same applies to our father. As a young man he was a successful business man known throughout the district, but by the time we were in our teens the family was in extreme poverty. The suffering we went through as children was unimaginable.

Suddenly our eyes were opened to this pattern in our lives. We realized that we were very young, but had already made a lot of money. We owned properties and drove some of the nicest cars available; but suddenly we had started losing money. As survival became increasingly difficult we started looking for the reason why and seeking a solution.

Cliff: Then in 2004 George got born-again in this house. Pastor Tom's teaching and instruction began to make sense and with the Word came the transformation. He brought me (Cliff) to church a year later when Apostle Gbenga was here and instructed people to bring someone to church. George had to really push me to come; I was very skeptical that this would help me, but coming to this church has been revolutionary. The principles that we have been taught have transformed our lives. We are the first generation that has known Christ in our family and we have faced extreme resistance. The ridicule and criticism is still coming; but our lifestyle and the maturity that we present especially at family gatherings is amazing a lot of relatives especially those that have not seen us for a couple of years.

Added to this is the fact that God has begun prospering both our immediate families, and the rest of the people can see this. To date 15 family members have come to know Christ.

At times other family members suggest that we remember the ancestors who are restoring our prosperity, but we know it is not them. It is because of the teaching on giving we have received in this house. Giving to the church was not a challenge to us, from the time we got plugged in to the vision we started giving as Pastor Tom instructed. At times the finances were not there, but when we desired to give to the vision the provision always came, and we gave with liberality and out of the abundance of our hearts. There was no fear in us, because there was no compulsion.

We realize that we still have a long way to go because of the extent of the family's involvement in the occult. We don't want to rest — we want to supersede the giving we did while worshiping ancestors. We have learned that this is about the generations that are coming. We want to build prosperity for the generations as taught by Pastor Tom.

George: When we made the decision to have our lives rotate around the church everything began to come into alignment. Our business has grown and we're now looking at expansion. I no longer just trade in agricultural commodities, but have expanded into manufacturing of stock feeds. If it wasn't for the principles that have been taught, none of this would have happened. The vision is broadening, I used to distribute soybeans — but now we get three products from the soybean!

We thank God for our Pastors and the message of reformation that they have brought to this nation.

There is no greater joy or honor than to be a part of the reason for change in our lives.

These powerful testimonies are lives radically changed by application of the principles of the Kingdom that we teach. This is the start of reformation, this is the beginning of national transformation, which is a process one person at a time.

Sacrifice to Penetrate

As much of the church has been lulled into comfort, and yet prays for reformation and relevance, we have forgotten our roots. Reformation and relevance do not come without great sacrifice. As I've studied the history of the great revivals, there were two elements that made them effective. One was prayer, but the other was sacrifice. The early pilgrims that went to America risked and sacrificed lands, fortunes and their lives, so that they could worship freely. The reformers in Europe risked their lives, many were burned at the stake and gave their fortunes, to own or even just to read, a segment of Scripture, not even a whole Bible! Circuit preachers would travel from town to town with no guarantee of offering or honorarium or even help, often being rejected and driven from their mission. Yet simply shaking the dust off their feet they would go on to the next town, and there see the power of God fall and revival come. The early Pentecostal and healing ministers paid terrible prices financially, emotionally and physically to bring truth to bear throughout the world. Today we have grown familiar, fat and comfortable and want a convenient Gospel. It is this false sense of security which must be loosened or the idolatry of greed will hinder the Kingdom's advance.

This is a very difficult message for people who love money because their vested interests are being threatened. This love of money hinders people in the Church from doing what God wants them to do and it cannot be broken without penetrating prayer.

Jesus' Life of Penetrating Prayer

This seems a hard message, but Jesus coaches His disciples in the area of finances and property to relax, to not be anxious. He reiterates again and again that if God clothes the lilies and the grass, then how much more will He clothe them. Jesus encourages His disciples to trust the Father for their provision. He sends them forth as givers and commands them to "provide yourselves money bags which do not grow old." Jesus gives us the key to this lifestyle, He says, "For where your treasure is, there your heart will be also."

Consider the lilies, how they grow: they neither toil nor spin; and yet I say to you, even Solomon in all his glory was not arrayed like one of these.

If then God so clothes the grass, which today is in the field and tomorrow is thrown into the oven, how much more *will He clothe you*, O *you* of little faith?

And do not seek what you should eat or what you should drink, nor have an anxious mind.

For all these things the nations of the world seek after, and your Father knows that you need these things.

But seek the kingdom of God, and all these things shall be added to you.

Do not fear, little flock, for it is your Father's good pleasure to give you the kingdom.

Sell what you have and give alms; provide your-selves money bags which do not grow old, a treasure in the heavens that does not fail, where no thief approaches nor moth destroys.

For where your treasure is, there your heart will be also.
                                            Luke 12:27-34 (NKJV)

Jesus' life was focused on His goal. He accomplished His purpose through meditating on the Scriptures and applying daily persevering prayer. His habit was to rise early and pray (Mark 1:35, Luke 5:16 NKJV). This persevering prayer is what Jesus had trained Himself in, and was ready to draw on in the Garden of Gethsemane. This tenacious relationship with the Father enabled Him to complete the most critical and difficult purpose God has ever tasked any-one with. Jesus' life truly depicts the greatest demonstra-tion of persevering prayer in the New Testament.

Paul's Pattern for Penetrating Prayer

Second to this is the Apostle Paul. The Apostle Paul is a driven man with a desire to extend God's Kingdom. He makes a decision to go to Asia and then is forbidden by the Holy Spirit to go to Asia. The reason for him being forbidden can be speculated on, but I think he was not ready to encounter the kind of demonic activity that was in the hearts and minds of the Asian world at that time. God begins to lead Paul, first by a vision and a call to the Macedonian church, and then through a series of encounters, teaching him how to penetrate cultures, and preparing him for his final conquest – Asia!

I've outlined both his first and second missionary journeys because I believe it is important to understand that he was being trained as he was going. Each city posed different problems and different spiritual entities. Paul confronted and was confronted. As he learned he was finally equipped to face the principalities in Asia. All of us are learning from our experiences and where we are being led into, from strength to strength, glory to glory, grace to grace, faith to faith.

Paul applies patterns and principles throughout his ministry. He:

- Targets key cities, centers of the known world, to start churches in.
- Starts preaching in Synagogues, and meeting with existing religious leadership first.
- Preaches the Gospel and multitudes of Jews, Greeks and prominent business people, men and women, believe.
- Experiences violent opposition from jealous Jews and Gentiles alike.
- Takes his direction from the Holy Spirit in full submission to the Jerusalem Church leadership.

68

Paul's First Missionary Journey: Galatia

Barnabus and Saul were sent from Antioch, a multi-national and multi-cultural church, birthed after the persecution that arose after the stoning of Stephen.

> **Now those who were scattered after the persecution that arose over Stephen traveled as far as Phoenicia, Cyprus, and Antioch, preaching the word to no one but the Jews only.**
>
> **But some of them were men from Cyprus and Cyrene [Africa], who, when they had come to Antioch, spoke to the Hellenists, preaching the Lord Jesus.**
>
> **And the hand of the Lord was with them, and a great number believed and turned to the Lord.**
>
> **Acts 11:19-21 (NKJV)**

Peter had convinced the Jerusalem church leadership that "God has also granted to the Gentiles repentance to life" (Acts 11:18), and because news of the "great number" believing in Antioch had reached the church in Jerusalem, they sent Barnabus to Antioch. Once at Antioch, Barnabus realized the church was in great need of teaching, a task which needed Saul. So he made the 100 mile journey to Tarsus to find Saul, brought him back to Antioch, and for a year together they *taught a great many people*. Here the disciples were "first called Christians" (Acts 11:26). Barnabus and Saul traveled to Jerusalem with a financial gift for the brethren, and after the supernatural death of Herod, they returned to Antioch with John Mark (Acts 12:25).

Now back in Antioch, the multicultural church leadership sent Barnabus and Paul out.

> **Now in the church that was at Antioch there were certain prophets and teachers: Barnabas [a Levite native of Cyprus], Simeon who was called Niger [possibly**

from Cyrene], **Lucius of Cyrene** [in Tripoli], **Manaen** [Rome] **who had been brought up with Herod the tetrarch, and Saul** [Tarsus].

Acts 13:1 (NKJV)

Note the number of nationalities represented at Antioch.

As they ministered to the Lord and fasted, the Holy Spirit said, "*Now separate to Me Barnabas and Saul for the work to which I have called them.*"

Then, having fasted and prayed, and laid hands on them, they sent them away.

So, being sent out by the Holy Spirit, they went down to Seleucia, and from there they sailed to Cyprus.

Acts 13:2-4 (NKJV)

Barnabus and Paul, with John Mark as assistant, preached in towns through the island of Cyprus (Barnabus' home). In each of the towns and cities they preached in, God used the situations to prepare Paul to go to Asia. Although in Paul's second journey God forbids Paul to go to Asia, it is evident that the workings of God in Paul's life were to prepare him for the work in the strongly held and contested city of the Goddess Diana, Ephesus, but before Paul could have dominion for the Gospel in Ephesus he needed to learn some valuable lessons.

I believe as we look at this summary of Paul's travels, it will forge a more profound revelation of just what it takes to achieve *penetrating breakthroughs*, of the sort that we desperately need worldwide today.

The first journey of almost 1,200 miles by foot and sea, after Cyprus, included Antioch, in Pisidia, which was a key mountain city ranked third in Roman Empire after Rome and Alexandria. Here Paul, as was his custom (Acts 17:2), and Jesus' custom (Luke 4:16), went to

Synagogue on the Sabbath. He was invited to *exhort* the people, and *many believed, but* the Jews were filled with envy (Acts 13:45), and had *Paul and Barnabus expelled* from the region.

> But *the Jews stirred up* the devout and prominent women and the chief men of the city, raised up persecution against Paul and Barnabas, and expelled them from their region.
>
> But they shook off the dust from their feet against them, and came to Iconium.   Acts 13:50,51 (NKJV)

The next city Iconium was the capital of ancient Lycaonia where a different language was spoken.

> Again Paul went to...the *synagogue,* and so spake, that a great *multitude* both of the Jews and also of the Greeks believed.   Acts 14:1 (KJV)
>
> But the *unbelieving Jews stirred* up the Gentiles and *poisoned their minds against* the brethren.
>
> [Although they spoke] *"boldly* in the Lord, Who was bearing witness to the word of His grace, granting *signs and wonders* to be done by their hands....
>
> ...the multitude of the city was divided: part sided with the Jews, and part with the apostles.
>
> And when a *violent attempt was made by both the Gentiles and Jews, with their rulers, to abuse and stone* them,
>
> they became aware of it and fled to Lystra and Derbe, cities of Lycaonia, and to the surrounding region.
>
> And they were preaching the gospel there.   Acts 14:2-7 (NKJV)

71

In the small town of Lystra, a wild district with a rude population, which was Timothy's home town, Paul and Barnabus *preached the Gospel* and a man who was a *cripple from his mother's womb*, heard Paul speaking.

Paul, observing him intently and seeing that he had faith to be healed,

said with a loud voice, "Stand up straight on your feet!" And he leaped and walked.

Acts 14:9,10 (NKJV)

At this the crowd tried to worship them with sacrifices, to Paul as Hermes [Mercury] and Barnabus as Zeus [Jupiter].

But when the apostles Barnabas and Paul heard this, they tore their clothes and ran in among the multitude, crying out and saying, "Men, why are you doing these things?"

Acts 14:14 (NKJV)

Strange as it then seems, the crowd then turned on the very men they were about to idolize and *stoned Paul*!

Then Jews from Antioch and Iconium came there; and having persuaded the multitudes, they stoned Paul and dragged him out of the city, supposing him to be dead.

However, when the disciples gathered around him, he rose up and went into the city.

Acts 14:19,20 (NKJV)

In the small town of Derbe, home of Gaius, who later became a church leader, Paul and Barnabus preached uneventfully and made many disciples.

Now here, at the *end of the road*, the last of the cities Paul intended to visit, is the remarkable decision. Paul and Barnabus did not take the easy route home, direct east from Derbe to Tarsus, to Antioch. They had preached in the face of huge opposition and had barely survived, but still they chose to return to these cities, Lystra, Iconium and Antioch, the very places they had nearly lost their lives! They were compelled to, "strengthen the souls of the disciples, exhorting them to continue in the faith, and saying, 'We must through many tribulations enter the kingdom of God'" (Acts 14:22).

They did not want to lose what they had struggled so hard to obtain! In order to establish their *first* work, they had to set in place church leadership, so they appointed elders, "So when they had appointed elders in every church, and prayed with fasting, they commended them to the Lord in whom they had believed." They then proceeded to report back to Antioch (Syria), "where they had been commended to the grace of God for the work which they had completed" (Acts 14:21-26). At all times Paul submitted to the authorities of the church and reported back to them at the conclusion of each journey. It is also evident that throughout each trip Paul is constantly guided by the Holy Spirit.

The new church had genuine doctrinal issues, so Paul and Barnabus were sent to *the apostles and elders* in Jerusalem to deal with the controversy about circumcision. A heated debate ensued,which was silenced as the apostles and elders heard about the miracles, signs and wonders wrought by Barnabus and Paul among the Gentiles. After this James settled the matter by reading from Amos 9:11,12, "so that the rest of mankind may seek the Lord," and proposes the letter to go to those from among the Gentiles who are turning to God.

Paul's Second Missionary Journey: Galatia and Macedonia

Paul understood the principle that as hard as it may have been to obtain both spiritual and natural ground, it would be just as hard to maintain the territory taken. Having achieved great strides for the Kingdom through applying bunker-busting prayer, he saw a bigger picture, and was therefore able to focus on what it would take to establish something that would be ongoing. His aim was not simply to make converts, but to mentor disciplined followers of Jesus Christ, trained to extend the Kingdom of God. This is why after having been beaten, left for dead, and threatened on his first journey, he was willing to go yet again to make sure that the territory gained was not lost.

Paul chose Silas to accompany him on this second journey, and also took Timothy with him from Lystra. As Paul set off on his second trip to the new churches to "see how they were doing" (Acts 15:36), and to strengthen them, he also brought instruction from the Church leadership's letter to these new churches.

And as they went through the cities, they delivered to them the decrees to keep, which were determined by the apostles and elders at Jerusalem.

So the churches were strengthened in the faith, and increased in number daily.
                                                    Acts 16:4-5

After passing through Syria, Cilicia, Phrygia and Galatia, modern day Syria and central Turkey, "they were forbidden by the Holy Spirit to preach the word in Asia" (Acts 16:6), today's western Turkey, where the city of Ephesus was the seat of the worship of Diana for the whole region. They then tried to go into Bythnia (north Turkey), "but the Holy Spirit did not permit them" (Acts 16:7). Both of these instances indicate that Paul constantly relied on the direction of the Holy Spirit to direct him. He had good plans, to evangelize Asia and Bynthnia, but the strategy he followed came from God. This is how bunker-busters work. The plans of God, spoken out and acted on by man. "The steps of a good man are ordered by the Lord" (Psalm 37:23).

[Bypassing these regions], **"a vision appeared to Paul in the night. A man of Macedonia** [modern day Greece] **stood and pleaded with him, saying, "Come over to Macedonia and help us."**

When he had seen the vision, immediately we sought to go into Macedonia, concluding that God had called us to preach the Gospel to them.

So, putting out to sea from Troas, we ran a straight course to Samothrace, and on the day following to Neapolis;

and from there to Philippi, which is a leading city of Macedonia.

Acts 16:9-12

Philippi

Once more Paul targets the major city, and the place of customary prayer, as there was no synagogue, "...on the Sabbath day we went out of the city to the riverside, where prayer was customarily made and we sat down and spoke to the women who met there" (Acts 16:13). A young slave girl possessed by a spirit of divination was there, and after Paul had cast out the demon (Acts 16:18), her owners seeing their profit go down the drain, dragged Paul and Silas to the magistrates who had them imprisoned. At midnight, Paul and Silas were "praying and singing hymns to God and the prisoners were listening to them." When suddenly an earthquake hit, the "prison foundations were shaken", immediately all the doors were opened and everyone's chains were loosed (Acts 16:26). Paul saves the prison warden and, "they spoke the word of the Lord to him and to all who were in his house. And he took them the same hour of the night and washed their stripes, and immediately he and all his family were baptized" (Acts 16:30-33). Although pleaded with by the authorities to leave the city, Paul did not leave before seeing and encouraging the brethren at Lydia's house.

Thessalonica

The pattern is repeated in Thessalonica, where Paul visits the synagogue, a great multitude of devout Greeks and leading women join Paul and Silas (Acts 17:4), the Jews become envious, stir up the city, attack the house where Paul is staying and Paul is immediately sent by night to Berea.

Berea

Once again in Berea they went to the synagogue where the people "received the Word with all readiness and searched the Scriptures daily…and many of them therefore believed, along with a number of prominent Greek women and men…" (Acts 17:11). Once more Paul experienced opposition from the Jews who came and stirred up the crowds (Acts 17:13), so Paul was conducted by sea to Athens.

Athens

In Athens Paul's spirit is provoked by the blatant idolatry, and he pursues the same pattern and procedure to his outreach as he has used to date, that of reasoning in the Synagogue, as well as daily in the market place, but shockingly the results he experiences are pitiful, just *some men* and *a woman*. The Word of God was *mocked* (Acts 17:32) here, a rejection which Jesus experienced in Nazareth, where he could do no miracles (Matthew 13:57,58). Of note is that the Areopagus was a place where "the Athenians and the foreigners who were there spent their time in nothing else but either to tell or to hear some new thing, rather like many today who spend hours watching the news on TV, the internet, listening to talk radio or reading the newspapers! The address Paul gives at the Areopagus is a treatise, a skillful and academic address, but only received a mild response from the people, who were full of the various philosophies of the times. "After these things Paul departed from Athens and went to Corinth" (Acts 18:1). There is no record in Athens of a body of believers, of persecution or of any spiritual activity of note!

What Paul discovered in Athens is probably one of the most significant church planting lessons in the New Testament. Initially Paul chose to try to match philosophy for philosophy and wit for wit by debating with the Epicureans and Stoics and strangers at the Areopagus on Mars Hill. Paul was virtually ineffective with the debate. Although the Scripture doesn't say so, I believe he probably learned his greatest lesson in terms of what it would take to bring reformation through his encounters on Mars Hill. He found out that it wasn't just effective preaching that was needed or persuasive arguments, but there was a need to deal with principalities and powers that held strongholds in men's minds.

In Athens Paul is drawn in to intellectual debate, he is trying to persuade people on their level. When he comes to Corinth we see that he has learned a great lesson as he declares how he came to them saying,

> When I came to you, brothers, I did not come with eloquence or superior wisdom as I proclaimed to you the testimony about God.
>
> For I resolved to know nothing while I was with you except Jesus Christ and him crucified.
>
> I came to you in weakness and fear, and with much trembling.

My message and my preaching were not with wise and persuasive words, but with a demonstration of the Spirit's power,

so that your faith might not rest on men's wisdom, but on God's power.

1 Corinthians 2:1-5 (NIV)

What Paul had lacked in Athens, had caused him to come to Corinth in weakness. This position of personal frailty was more than compensated for as he preached the Word only, and demonstrated its power, and so had penetration. God gave Paul a personal word to strengthen and encourage him, "the Lord spoke to Paul in the night by a vision, 'Do not be afraid, but speak, and do not keep silent; for I am with you, and no one will attack you to hurt you; for I have many people in this city', and he continued there a year and six months, teaching the word of God among them" (Acts 18:9,10).

After Paul's lessons in Corinth, he finally was allowed to go to Asia. This was the first time he wasn't removed from a city violently. The lesson he learned in Corinth equipped him for Ephesus, now he is prepared to take on the demonic stronghold of Diana.

When he came to Ephesus, on his third missionary journey, he had been equipped, and was used by God to break the back of spiritual power in that city and the region, Diana of the Ephesians. As he had done in Corinth, Paul started "reasoning and persuading concerning the things of the Kingdom of God" in the synagogue, but when some rejected this teaching, he left them and withdrew the disciples, "reasoning daily in the school of Tyrannus" (Acts 19:9), for a further two years.

This is now a defining period of Paul's ministry, "God worked unusual miracles by the hands of Paul" (Acts 19:11). Healings and deliverances occurred, which brought a new level of authority to Paul, "fear fell on them all, and the name of the Lord Jesus was magnified" (Acts 19:17). Many came publicly destroying all connection with witchcraft, burning their books to the tune of fifty thousand pieces of silver! "So The word of the Lord grew mightily and prevailed" (Acts 19:20). This was a spontaneous and public repentance of occult involvement, a deliverance amongst believers, and a breakthrough in Paul's ministry. Although Paul faced one of the fiercest conflicts of his life in Ephesus, the riotous crowd headed up by Alexander the silversmith was not able to drive him out, the crowd was dismissed and Paul peacefully took his leave of the disciples.

Every place that Paul went before Ephesus, with the exception of Corinth, he was actually driven from the city, or was beaten or persecuted greatly for his preaching, but in each of those places God was teaching him and he was adding weapons to his arsenal that would eventually allow him to penetrate, and take dominion.

What we can learn from this, is that God is desiring us as individuals and corporately, to actually advance and take ground for His Kingdom, and He is teaching us many lessons along the way if we're willing to learn them, but we cannot learn them in the "comfort zone."

Penetrating Prayer Through Praying in Tongues

Earlier in the book I mentioned that praying in tongues in corporate prayer can often be a *cop-out* for effective surgical prayer. I would like to qualify the idea and raise the importance of praying in tongues in the individual's life to the highest level. Praying in tongues actually helps the individual believer with his effectiveness in corporate prayer. When we pray in tongues, the Bible says that "we edify ourselves" (1 Corinthian 14:4), "we speak mysteries to God" (1 Corinthians 14:2b) and "we build ourselves up in our most holy faith, praying in the spirit" (Jude 20). The benefits of praying in tongues cannot be underestimated in both personal and corporate prayer. The Apostle Paul also says that we must pray in the spirit and pray with our understanding, "I will pray with the spirit, and I will also pray with the understanding. I will sing with the spirit, and I will also sing with the understanding" (1 Corinthians 14:15b).

If a believer is built up in the Holy Spirit, that is to say that he has prayed to where faith is high and the believer is listening for the interpretation of what he is praying in the Spirit, can you imagine how powerful his prayers will be and how strong his faith will be in corporate prayer! The Apostle Paul said, "I thank my God I speak with tongues more than you all" (1 Corinthians 14:18), and his life was not short of power!

Many ask why we don't see power in our corporate prayer meetings. I have noticed that when people who have powerful personal prayer lives join together in corporate prayer, the quality and power of their prayers affects the corporate meeting and is marked by supernatural activity and answers. I don't believe we will see the miracles, the breakthrough and the penetration that we are looking for with corporate prayer only lasting 15 minutes before a Sunday service. There will have to be a "sacrifice" of prayer.

Chapter 5
Surgical Prayer is Purposeful

Domain prayer allows for the diversity of age, gender, and temperament to gather together and focus *all manner of prayer* in a specific direction. There is much teaching today about purpose when it comes to directing our lives, churches, businesses even nations. When it comes to prayer, some of the same rules of logic and the disciplines that guide purpose-led people seem to break down. In fact, many people move into a surreal and magical world when they begin to pray.

Purpose is derived from the Latin "propositum, propono; pro, before, and pono, to set or place" (Webster Dictionary). It's definition is, "That which a person sets before himself as an object to be reached or accomplished; the end or aim to which the view is directed in any plan, measure or exertion. To intend; to design; to resolve; to determine on some end or object to be accomplished."

I believe that purposeful prayer has four dimensions to it:

1) It is firmly based in reality and works within well-defined parameters. It understands governmental authority surrounding the domains in which it is being applied.

2) While founded in reality, purposeful prayer is able to lift its eyes and visualize the outcomes as well as verbalize what we see.

3) The over-riding purpose of domain prayer is to extend God's Kingdom on earth.

4) Purposeful prayer must always have the element of corresponding activity in the sphere and domain to which the prayers are being directed.

Let me expand on these four points.

Based in Reality

Once you set forth in domain prayer you soon begin to realize that there are rules of engagement for each domain. It is important to have knowledge, both historical and current, concerning the areas you are engaging, in order to launch from a foundation of reality. The more informed someone is, or the more the domain touches their lives personally, the more effective and accurate their prayers will be. As we gathered to pray we covered our five day week by assigning common interests to each of the days, each area of interest we called a *domain*. This attracted those knowledgeable in their area of dominion. Immediately we noticed a heightened fervor and focus in prayer as the majority of those gathering could now identify with the prayer and become fully involved in the process of prayer.

Spiritual Protocol

Having set in place the domain days of prayer, we also realized the need for an understanding of the governmental authority surrounding the domains in which we were praying. Whilst not being familiar with the specific protocols used by national governments, we were aware that they existed. These are protocols in the natural world that cannot be broken. For example, when you present yourself before a president of a nation, there are certain clearances, procedures and behaviors which must be observed before you gain an audience. Likewise protocols exist in the spiritual world, set in place by God.

For by him all things were created: things in heaven and on earth, visible and invisible, whether thrones or powers or rulers or authorities; all things were created by Him and for Him. Colossians 1:16 (NIV)

God has prescribed certain protocols to follow in our approach to Him. For example in the Psalms He said we must, "enter His gates with thanksgiving and His courts with praise" (Psalm 100:4). In the New Testament Jesus teaches His disciples to pray, beginning with, "Our Father in heaven, Hallowed be Your Name. Your kingdom come, Your will be done on earth as it is in heaven" (Matthew 6:9,10). When we enter the Father's presence we acknowledge His authority and position, then we acclaim Him. We understand that we have been made worthy to stand boldly before Him in the Name of His Son, because the price of our redemption, the shed blood of the Lamb, has been paid.

But God demonstrates His own love toward us, in that while we were still sinners, Christ died for us.

Much more then, having now been justified by His blood, we shall be saved from wrath through Him.

For if when we were enemies we were reconciled to God through the death of His Son, much more, having been reconciled, we shall be saved by His life. Romans 5:8-10 (NKJV)

A part of this protocol includes having people with the appropriate level of authority in the correct positions in the prayer meetings. Not all people in corporate prayer carry the same authority, either in life or in the spirit. Even Jesus taught that He gave different gifts and talents to different people, and therefore varying degrees of authority and responsibility (Luke 12:48). We realized we needed to set in place an appropriate structure for our meetings. As we set out well-defined parameters, we noticed the stability and focus of each meeting increased, commensurate with a growth in numbers attending. We appointed prayer leaders for each domain, and they grew teams around them. The appointed leaders were sensitive in the spirit and would strongly lead the direction the meetings went in. They had authority over who had access to the microphone. Less time was wasted on the immature prophetic words or vague, unrelated prayers. Prayer became focused and powerful. Testimonies of corporate answered prayer galvanized further prayer and glorified God in our midst. Everyone who came felt they had corporately accomplished something useful with the time. Leaders in society in each domain were now coming as they gained revelation of the power of corporate prayer in their domain.

One of the examples I like to tell my congregation, of the need for prayer to be based in reality, is of a young university student who came to prayer for three days in a row, and each day kept boasting that he would become the Minister of Transport for the nation. After the third day of his incessant boasting I grabbed him by the collar and said, "Come with me!" I took him to the parking lot and asked him to show me his car. Needless to say, as we walked to it, his shoulders began to droop and I knew I was on the right track. When we arrived at his car, the first thing I noticed was that it was filthy. Secondly the tires on the back of the car were threadbare, even the metal belts were showing through. I pointed out his front tires were wearing badly because he had a toe-in problem and probably hadn't replaced his shock absorbers. I then proceeded to ask him to open the trunk of his car. Words cannot describe the lack of order and the amount of grease, oil and old spare parts strewn about the trunk of his car. Yet there was no car jack or spare tire, nothing for safety, and the carpet that had once covered the back was in tatters.

Moving to the interior of the car, as he opened the door, the smell of moldy left-over fast-foods was overpowering. The back seat and under the seats were littered with no less than twenty take-out packages with varying degrees of left-over food in them! Coke bottles were freely spread about the vehicle and there was a fine layer of oily, greasy, sticky substance mixed with dust and dirt all over the dashboard and steering wheel of the car. Finally, there were gaping holes in the dashboard of the vehicle where there had been radios and air-conditioning units in the past. I looked at this young man and I said, "If you were going to be the minister of transport, and this is how you take care of your own personal vehicle, then how do you think you will manage the nation's fleets of trucks and buses, aircraft, railways, road systems and the like!!" My goal was not to shame the young man but to help him base his life and his prayers in reality. This was a wake-up call for him.

We began to talk often to our young people about baseless boasting. One of the sayings that we soon adopted was that, "if you are a lizard in Zimbabwe, you will not be a crocodile in London." This is more important than anyone will ever know when it comes to prayer. Often our prayers can be based in a fantasy or a dream, a wild leap of faith with no basis or possibility of even being answered. Prayer has as much to do with the character of the person praying, as with the prayers being prayed, when it comes to the kind of prayer that will lead us to reformation and transformation of a nation. We've come to realize that God expects us to be part of the solution for the prayers that we are praying. If we do not have this same revelation, we will frustrate the plans of God to bring solutions into our domains.

Another example of the need for our prayers to be based in reality and why many people fail to see the manifestation of their prayers, is best illustrated by a Bible study and prayer meeting I used to lead during the War of Liberation in Zimbabwe. On one occasion I went out to the farmers and told them if they prayed and believed for rain, they would receive rain. I could tell some of them really caught this and we all stood and held hands to pray. They were praying and they were saying, "we believe and we receive now." I thought they had really understood it.

However, ten minutes after our fervent prayers, we were sipping tea, and I overheard a farmer saying, " Have you noticed how the weavers are building their nests low in the trees? That is a sure sign of drought. Have you noticed the cloud formations? Those are the Botswana highs, a sure sign that the rain will not be coming soon." So I just walked up to them and calmly said, "let's talk about believing and receiving. Do you guys really believe what you prayed, or do you believe more in the weavers and the Botswana highs?" They saw it. They realized that they actually believed more in what they saw, and sensed, than in what they prayed and believed. If you believe and receive you don't have to keep requesting, you just keep thanking God and affirming the answer.

Visualize and Verbalize The Outcomes

As we pray surgically on purpose, we must understand it is not always about believing for extraordinary or notable things to happen, or to be received. Although from time to time the extraordinary and notable does

happen. Advances that have long-lasting effects in reformation, usually come about by taking out or putting in
place a Biblical world view one component at a time,
through surgical prayer. All change takes place one person at a time from the inside out. However the notable
does also occur.

In the early days of my ministry in Zimbabwe I
found myself risking my life on a number of occasions
driving on roads that had been land-mined. I felt my
prayers being directed towards what seemed at the time
to be impossible for me to grasp. I began to visualize
myself flying an aircraft into different towns and even
onto some of the farms that I was ministering at. This
was very far-fetched for a young missionary who was
barely making ends meet! However the vision was strong
and my confession was powerful. I even put a picture of
an aircraft on my refrigerator door. Through a series of
events God began to deal with me and teach me about
the power of visualizing and believing for the desires He
would place in my heart.

As things worked out, I had to make a hasty trip to
the USA and was unable to schedule any preaching
engagements there, but once I arrived, a number of small
Bible Studies and churches invited me to share my mission. At a small Bible-study in the south of Denver there
was a young man who interrupted me in the middle of
my preaching and asked me if I needed an airplane! As I
pulled out the list of things I was believing for, I told the
young man, "As a matter of fact, the first thing on my list
is an airplane!" I went on to tell him that I kept a list at
the back of my Bible, so I just read him the list right from
the top; "airplane, car, typewriter, and audio tape
recorder." As I finished my message and closed the meeting, that man came to me and in a very apologetic tone

saying, "I am sorry for interrupting you like that, but God was speaking to me right then and I didn't know what to do." He explained that God told him to give me money for an airplane. He was thrilled and so was I, as he signed a check for the value of the plane.

The principle is that the need was urgent, it was based in reality, and as I visualized and verbalized, my surgical prayer was answered in a seemingly dramatic way. In reality God was not only teaching me His laws of provision, but had an assignment that required the use of an airplane. This assignment could not have been carried out, had I not asked and believed specifically for the airplane, and then received God's provision.

Bunker-Buster Prayer

I've spoken about the impact of praying in domains, and about praying surgical prayer in those domains. One type of surgical prayer I mentioned earlier, which is the most powerful and precise, is what we have begun to call *bunker-buster* prayer.

Because of the constant onslaught of chaos and problems we face in Zimbabwe, we have had to learn to stop praying about the problems we constantly face, and to stop trying to correct those problems in prayer. We learned that when we pray about a problem, we are focusing on the problem. We came to understand as we do that, without realizing it, we are attracting the problem to ourselves and amplifying the problem.

Take for example gossip. If I come to you and say, "Did you know the Collins family look like nice people, but I know for a fact that they never pay their bills!" I've just planted that little seed of doubt about their character in your mind. What happens the next time you see the Collins family? When you start communicating with them, you are not attracting the best out of them. In fact, the words I've spoken to you have created a judgment in you which causes you to think, "I'd better be careful of those people, my pastor wasn't real complimentary of them."

We attract to ourselves the things that we speak about, whether it's about ourselves, others or the nation. It's not long before we witness the attribute we speak about manifesting in our lives, because what we believe and speak is what we attract. The character of a person may not be anything like the negative report we've spoken about, although they may have a weakness in that area, but if you focus on weakness, you'll always get weakness. Meanwhile you're missing out on the five hundred strengths that they have, because all you can see is the weakness. So it is with prayer of all sorts.

There was a time in our church when we used to pray about racial issues. This used to be a significant problem in the church, with one race being antagonistic to another. It always used to amaze me that when we prayed about the racial concerns, the people that prayed the longest and the hardest, would experience the most difficulty in this area. It seems like the people that talked the most about racial problems had the greatest difficulty functioning in a multi-racial setting. Why? Because what you focus on is what you attract to yourself. What you see, what you look at, is what you're going to get. Do you understand that?

So then, let me explain how the *bunker-buster* works. When we start praying in our domains, such as education, we don't speak about the problems in our schools, or about the problems with education, instead we start visualizing and praying what the Kingdom of God looks like. Being fully aware of the problems, we choose to look for the heavenly picture of how it should be. Jesus said, "Thy kingdom come, Thy will be done on earth as it is in Heaven." How is it structured in heaven? What is the heavenly pattern? What is it that you see? Because if you talk about the problem, that becomes your focus. Let us rather proclaim the answer. This is not to deny the problem, but I'm saying, let us decree into the situation, God's solution.

I can show you throughout the Bible that that is exactly what God does. Jesus brought people to a realization of the solution. For example, one day when he was walking along a road, two blind men cried out, "Have mercy on us, O Lord, Son of David" (Matthew 20:30 NIV)! Not a bad prayer is it? It's a carpet-bombing type of prayer. "Have mercy." What does that mean? Are you feeling sorry for yourself? Are you a victim? This is an exclamation of despair and a cry for attention, but this does not articulate what the men want. A carpet bombing prayer can get the attention of God.

I have heard all kinds of these prayers. For example, "We're in Zimbabwe! O God, have mercy on us! God how much more can we handle? Can't you see how desperate the situation is?" We act as though God does not see where we are at, or where we live, or what's going on around us. He knows our situation exactly!

So how does Jesus respond to the blind men? Listen to what Jesus says, "Jesus stopped and called them. 'What do you want me to do for you?'" I think He was really asking, "What exactly do you want?" "What is it that you really want?" Listen to their response. They spoke with faith, they declared a *bunker-buster*, "Lord, 'we want our sight.' Jesus had compassion on them and touched their eyes. Immediately they received their sight and followed him" (Matthew 20:32-34 NIV).

"We want to see." They didn't say, "Heal my blindness." Did you get that? They didn't talk about what they had; they didn't say, "I'm blind, heal my blindness." They simply said, "We want to see." Jesus said, "Hey, I can help you. I can do that." Had they said, "Heal my blindness" I don't know that they could have attracted the power of God, because they would have been focusing on their blindness!

My passionate intention is to help people pray powerfully and effectively, because the more of this type of prayer that we all engage in, the more rapid the expansion of the Kingdom of God will be. That is the heart of God, and is what Jesus reiterated throughout His ministry. *The Kingdom* is mentioned 150 times in the New Testament alone, over 90% of which were spoken by the Lord Jesus. Whilst prayers pleading with God for mercy are a valid part of *all manner of prayer*, they are a type of *carpet bomb* prayer. We can get smarter and rather use the *bunker-buster* type of prayer. As we get focused on seeing God's solutions, we will start attracting God's answers to ourselves. God knows our problems, just as Jesus knew that the two men were blind. Blind men had to wear a particular outfit, use a specific stick and exhibit certain behavior denoting they were blind. So Jesus knew they were blind, but it is only when they moved from the carpet bomb type of prayer, "Have mercy on us!" to, "We would see," That Jesus could respond with, "I can help you."

It's like the person who wants to lose weight. As long as they focus on losing weight they are going to get fat, because they are attracting weight to themselves. When the focus is weight, regardless of how hard they work to lose weight, the fatter they'll get. Weight is the issue, therefore every opportunity that comes along, the mental imagery says, "I'm losing weight. I'm on a diet."

Since what we look at is what we attract, and the focus is on weight, it will remain an internal issue and we will attract weight to ourselves. It is a principle that applies not only in the negative but in the positive as well. So when our strategy changes and we start to talk instead about a good quality of life and excellent health and fitness, and start visualizing what it is that we want to be, then there's no problem losing weight. What we see is what we attract.

Another critical area where we can see this demonstrated, is in our relationships. Take for example one of the most important relationships in society, husbands and wives. If a husband looks at his wife and all he sees is her faults, guess what he will keep noticing? Yes, he will see the fault manifested! The more he criticizes, even if he thinks he says it *nicely*, if he is speaking about the fault, guess what he will attract? He is going to keep attracting the faults, but when he can see beyond and lifts up his eyes to see the values and virtues in his wife, when he sees the Kingdom perspective of her, and starts to speak of her values and virtue instead of focusing on the faults, his wife will be stunned. She will become a different person. Some people are trapped, not because they are evil, but because of judgments that are held against them.

As we begin to see differently, we will decree differently and our prayers will be answered differently, hopefully with more accuracy and power.

Extending the Kingdom

I have just mentioned seeing a Kingdom perspective. What do I mean by that. In order to extend the Kingdom of God, we need to understand what the Kingdom of God is.

Firstly, we need to understand that we not only influence, but can be influenced by others. We need to realize that our prayers and thoughts, as well as those of others are powerful. That's why the Bible instructs us, "Don't hang around an angry man." Why is this? "Lest you learn his ways" (Proverbs 22:24,25). The Bible also teaches us, "Don't gossip." Why? Because it's a destruction to you, even to listen to a gossip is a destruction to you (Proverbs 26:22). How many good relationships have been broken because of gossip? We can traffic in that low level if we want to, but there's another level we are called to live at called the *Kingdom of God*. This is where our thinking is transformed (Romans 12:2), and our prayers and our corresponding actions are powerful for the pulling down of strongholds (2 Corinthians 10:4,5), and the building up and planting of nations (Jeremiah 1:10).

The key type of prayer to accomplish this is the *bunker-buster*, or the prayer of faith. When we live at this level there is nothing that can resist us. Suddenly when we pray, our prayers are answered.

Our outlook changes because we are operating in this high level of vision. The ability to remain at this level, or at any given level, is developed as we consciously determine to remain in "the Kingdom of God." This means that we must understand that the Kingdom of God is not a place but a disposition. In Romans 14:17 (NKJV) the apostle Paul says:

for the kingdom of God is not eating and drinking, but righteousness peace and joy in the Holy Spirit.

It takes a lot of love to see the good in everybody. It takes a lot of faith. It takes a lot of joy. We have to be genuinely happy to just stay up there, but you know what? Life just gets better, our prayers get answered, pretty soon we are saying, "You know what? I can't afford to leave the Kingdom disposition anymore. Excuse me, I can't agree with that prayer. Go ahead and ask for your blindness to be healed, but I'm going to ask for sight."

We need to start picturing what heaven really looks like in each domain. We must begin to declare heaven's vision as our own. Remember a *bunker busting* prayer is spoken in the present tense, not the future. It is a detailed and energetic visualization of what we see existing in heaven and we know by faith will be realized on earth.

Visualization Applied

Let me give you a practical example of a *bunker busting* prayer I am currently praying that pertains to the education domain:

As I drive into our Celebration Centre I see a beautiful three-story building over on my left. We have a special permit from the government to build at that height; I love the fact that they gave us that permit. That building stands there as a testimony of God's goodness. It's glass frontage reflects the Celebration Centre sanctuary as it stands as tall as the Centre and almost mirrors its design. The lines and elegance of this education building are striking, the color radiant and the surrounds are skillfully laid out to create a tranquil view from all sides of the school. Inside there are the acoustically perfect practice rooms for our musicians in the music school section. Upstairs we have comfortable, well equipped offices for all of our teachers and instructors. I love the lecture theatre with an amphitheater feel. We have all kinds of beautiful classrooms for our junior school students, and I can visualize the students enthusiastically studying and discovering the Kingdom, the world and the universe.

Our university is also housed there. It has a world-class, state of the art library with all the most up to date IT equipment and facilities. There's a little cafeteria area where the teachers can sit down and comfortably grade papers, and the adjacent administration block is fully staffed with highly skilled manpower. I thank God for it. I'm overwhelmed and totally energized that our education reformation is impacting the city and the nation and that students and teachers come from all over Africa and the world to be a part of what God is doing.

What do you see? What do you see for your family? "I see my sons like olive trees around my table. They rise up and they call me blessed. My sons and daughters, they're like arrows in my quiver, I can shoot them where I want to. My wife is a Proverbs 31 woman."

What do you see? Do you see, "Oh, God could you just get my wife to not nag me for one more day?" Guess what you're going to have for breakfast, lunch and dinner? Will you stay in the place of "Oh, Lord, can you heal my blindness?" or move to "Oh Lord, I would receive sight." We need to start visualizing and painting pictures with our understanding, declaring what our Kingdom families look like and "Calling those things that are not as though they are" (Romans 4:17 NIV). We need to take all the limitations off, pull out all the stops and communicate with God. We need to speak in a known tongue at this point and personalize and speak out Scriptures, because "God's Word never returns void" (Isaiah 55:11). We shouldn't be afraid to use the imaginations God has given us for this very purpose. We've been made in His image and likeness (Genesis 1:26 NKJV), with His creative power resident within us and have been mandated to go and do more than Jesus Himself did (John 14:12 NKJV)! What you can see, believe and say you can have (John 14:14 NKJV), that is how the Kingdom works.

In our nation I'm praying bunker-busters all the time. When I see somebody mistreating another person, I pray right there, "Father I thank you for a land where people honor and respect each other. I thank you, I see that we trust each other, we love each other." If I see a black person being abused by a white person, I say, "Father I thank you that our racial differences have been buried. I thank you Lord that we really do have genuine relationships between the races." If I see somebody scream out obscenities, I say, "I thank you Lord for a demonstration of self-control in public places." We are the force for good, the force to counteract the evil every-where we go; in our offices when there's an injustice, we drop a *bunker-buster*. In every instance I am willing to follow my prayers with appropriate action. We may not be able to go to the boss and say, "Hey, you're wrong." What we can do is start visualizing what it's going to look like as the Kingdom comes in that office, because the Kingdom is coming. That is why we are there.

In our schools and classrooms, sometimes those little kids just need a bunker-buster. They are facing terrible situations they can't deal with at home, so you begin to help them visualize what the Kingdom of God looks like. Help them to see, say and pray.

God operates this way, He told Abraham to, "Lift up your eyes now and look from the place where you are" (Genesis 13:14). God was trying to take his eyes off the situation and show him his future, His kingdom. God works the same way with us, what do we see? Many of us have just become so negative; we've become just like the world. We see the world news, we see the world's falling apart, we read the newspapers, we listen to the news and pretty soon that's all we see. Do you know what I see? I see a nation of righteous people rising up, a nation within a nation. I see the Kingdom of God being established that nobody will be able to gainsay against.

Visualization is a vital step to answered prayer that is only surpassed by action. It is a prerequisite to successful action, but a waste of time without corresponding action.

Corresponding Action

After the visualization and verbalization, purposeful prayer needs persevering action. When we watch concert pianists, Olympic gymnasts or Grand Slam tennis players, all experts in their field, we understand they didn't get there over night! Occasionally we've seen very young virtuosos, playing all the classics on the piano exquisitely, deftly and with apparent ease. They will have started practicing at a very young age, and perhaps by the age of six, they would be practicing six to eight hours a day, and that is what it has taken for them to become an expert. We don't become experts over night. People who have become experts have had to give up a lot of their unrelated interests.

To be an expert in the flow and things of the spirit many of us may have to make decisions to give up some legitimate things in life and make sacrifices for the things of God, but the price that we will pay will be insignificant when compared ultimately with the outcome. Prayer pays good dividends, and the more dividends I have received, the more I have been stirred again in my spirit to pray.

Another area in which this is extremely practical, yet we apply no logic to, is when we pray for people to get healed. Frequently either when we ask for prayer, or someone asks for prayer for healing, we don't connect our actions with our disease. We are filling our bodies with all sorts of food which act as poisons to our bodies, causing all kinds of sicknesses, and then we come to God and ask Him to heal us. It is as bizarre as purposely breaking our leg, then asking for prayer for God to heal it, and in God's mercy if He does heal us, how can we maintain that healing if our actions don't change?

When we make mistakes we must not give up, just get up and start again. I say *when* because we all need to understand the importance of persevering. Throughout the Scriptures God has explicitly recorded the failings of His mighty men, men like Moses and David and Peter, as well as detailing how they got up and continued by God's grace and mercy to complete the race set for them. God desires for our prayers to be answered and that we learn to move in His authority.

All prayer has purpose, so there are different purposes for each of the different types of prayer included in *all manner of prayer*. This includes prayers of thanksgiving, supplication, faith, intercession, *carpet bombing* and *bunker busting*! We have a multi-dimensional aspect of prayer in the Church and should not get stuck with one facet of prayer. God is multi-dimensional, so too is prayer. It is not only tongues or intercession or supplication, or the prayer of faith. There is another type of prayer as well, which helps us to live in the Kingdom. If we want to maintain our disposition of right thinking, peace and joy, we must be constantly aware of the presence of God. Brother Lawrence, a Roman Catholic monk wrote a simple booklet called, *Practicing the Presence of God*, which I recommend to anyone who is serious about living in the Kingdom of God and praying surgical prayers.

Testimony: Dr. Makoni

The main thing about prayer is to pray! We should be a symphony of prayer as we all take on various roles and express different types of prayer. The purpose of prayer isn't the form, it is the focus that is holistic and allows us to accomplish the purpose for which we are praying, which is to extend the Kingdom of God. We will deal more on this in the next chapter, but I would like you to hear Dr. Makoni's testimony. Dr. Makoni is a dental surgeon who is very actively involved in our church, and has just started to pastor our church in Bulawayo, the second largest city in Zimbabwe. You will see as he and his wife and family have made choices to get actively involved in various and many aspects of our vision, how God has built him and his family and built their dreams. They are part of lives being transformed and the nation being reformed.

Dr. Makoni shares:

My family and I joined Celebration Church on May 1, 2001 after transferring from a strong Pentecostal church. We sensed that God had spoken to us to move to Celebration Church, after we had faithfully served in the former church for almost twenty years. The Lord had intimated that for our growth to the next level in our business and ministry we needed this move.

We were there for the inauguration of the domain prayers each week day in the early morning, and we determined to be a part of what God was doing. We started attending the Monday morning (business domain) and the Thursday morning (Health Science and Technology domain). With the passage of time we added the Wednesday (Family and Education domain) sessions. Although we had to wake up earlier and drive some 75kms to attend the 0630hrs prayer sessions, we thoroughly enjoyed it. Our prayer life took a new dimension particularly because we were praying in a focused way about things that were close to our hearts. The beauty of the domain prayers is that they bridge the gap between your Sunday ministry and your marketplace ministry. Praying about issues in my profession and my areas of interest reignited my passion for prayer. I felt rejuvenated.

Through our involvement in prayer God opened doors of service for us in ways that blew our minds away. Through faithfulness, commitment and consistency in unexpected ways through a series of unexplainable events, God increased our ministry involvement. This took us by surprise as we had been *counseled* by our previous mentor that the move to Celebration Church would dwarf us as there were too many people serving and therefore we would not be effective! We grew spiritually and ministerially in a way we never thought possible. The apostolic gifting in Pastor Tom created a platform for us to serve effectively. Indeed we have grown both in our business and in our ministry to the saints.

Since we credit all this growth to domain prayers we have consistently engaged in the domain prayers as well as the all-night prayer sessions. We thank God for revealing the strategy of surgical domain prayers to Pastor Tom and for his boldness to release it into the Church. Our lives have never been the same. Our prayer lives are more effective and we enjoy the prayer meetings. It sounds strange, but we have over the years attended some really boring prayer meetings. Focused surgical prayers have really taken away the "bore" in prayer and intercession.

PART THREE

Patterns for Transformation

"Corporate transformational prayer is characterized by, and accomplished with, a spiritually alert, dynamic, focused, persevering prayer strategy, directed by apostolic church leadership."

Tom Deuschle

Chapter 6
Surgical Prayer is Prescriptive

When I think of being prescriptive in prayer, it has to do with the framework in which we pray. In terms of specific results, guidelines for prayer act as a scaffolding ensuring that our specific prayers are built into lasting edifices. By definition in medicine, to *prescribe* means: to lay down rules of medicinal usage. In other words, to prescribe the quantity of medicine per body weight, administered at set intervals for a specified duration, with an anticipated positive outcome or benefit.

The word *prescribe* is taken from the Latin word *proescribo* which means, *to write before*. Its use includes the following meanings, "to set or lay down authoritatively for direction; to give as a rule of conduct; as, to prescribe laws or rules. To direct; to give law; to influence arbitrarily; to influence by long use" (Webster's Dictionary).

Prescriptive prayer therefore contains aspects of time, intervals and duration, including the various aspects or contents required to obtain the set goal. Ultimately the manner in which we pray must bring about the desired result. To pray the same prayer and expect to get a different result is delusion or fantasy. If an athlete persists in playing the game the same way he has always done, regardless of the coach's instruction, he will never change the outcome of his game. It is necessary for us to take stock of how we are praying and the results we are obtaining, and where appropriate, change the manner in which we are praying.

From the definition above, *prescribe* also includes an aspect of the duration of application. That means it is not just a *once-off*, or prayer applied only during a prayer meeting. In the same way as the effectiveness of a medication can only be seen when it has been taken regularly and for the duration specified, this type of prayer has a life application. We have been instructed to, "pray always" (Luke 21:36, 2 Thessalonians 1:11). Prescriptive prayer must therefore entail a lifestyle application, it applies to our way of thinking, of speaking, of doing, in short, our character. When the various aspects that make up our lives are weighed up and applied, do they reflect and advance the prayers we are praying?

Again as with a medical prescription which is illness-specific, the strategy of prescriptive prayer is situation-specific. Jesus employed diverse actions on each occasion that He healed, so too God has a prayer strategy which is specific for each situation we need to influence with the Kingdom.

Lessons in Prayer from the Young Hebrew Boys

There are many stories in the Bible that describe what I call, being prescriptive in prayer. Shadrach, Meshach and Abednigo responded to Nebuchadnezzar's challenge with what I would term *prescriptive prayer*.

"Now when you hear the sound of the horn, flute, zither, lyre, harp, pipes and all kinds of music, if you are ready to fall down and worship the image I made, very good. But if you do not worship it, you will be

thrown immediately into a blazing furnace. Then what god will be able to rescue you from my hand?"

Shadrach, Meshach and Abednego replied to the king, "O Nebuchadnezzar, we do not need to defend ourselves before you in this matter.

If we are thrown into the blazing furnace, the God we serve is able to save us from it, and he will rescue us from your hand, O king.

But even if he does not, we want you to know, O king, that we will not serve your gods or worship the image of gold you have set up."

Then Nebuchadnezzar was furious with Shadrach, Meshach and Abednego, and his attitude towards them changed."

Daniel 3:15-19 (NIV)

Their statement to Nebuchadnezzar was their affirmation that reflected their prayer and their faith. They not only declared that God would answer their prayer, but that they were committed to their word and God's Word. Their apparent defiance of Nebuchadnezzar's decree set in motion God's answer.

"Then Nebuchadnezzar was furious with Shadrach, Meshach and Abednego, and his attitude towards them changed. He ordered the furnace to be heated seven times hotter than usual

and commanded some of the strongest soldiers in his army to tie up Shadrach, Meshach and Abednego and throw them into the blazing furnace.

So these men, wearing their robes, trousers, turbans and other clothes, were bound and thrown into the blazing furnace.

The king's command was so urgent and the furnace so hot that the flames of the fire killed the soldiers who took up Shadrach, Meshach and Abednego, and these three men, firmly tied, fell into the blazing furnace.

Then King Nebuchadnezzar leaped to his feet in amazement and asked his advisers, "Weren't there three men that we tied up and threw into the fire?" They replied, "Certainly, O king."

He said, "Look! I see four men walking around in the fire, unbound and unharmed, and the fourth looks like a son of the gods."

Nebuchadnezzar then approached the opening of the blazing furnace and shouted, "Shadrach, Meshach and Abednego, servants of the Most High God, come out! Come here! So Shadrach, Meshach and Abednego came out of the fire.

and the satraps, prefects, governors and royal advisers crowded around them. They saw that the fire had not harmed their bodies, nor was a hair of their heads singed; their robes were not scorched, and there was no smell of fire on them."

Then Nebuchadnezzar said, "Praise be to the God of Shadrach, Meshach and Abednego, who has sent his angel and rescued his servants! They trusted in him and defied the king's command and were willing to give up their lives rather than serve or worship any god except their own God.

Therefore I decree that the people of any nation or language who say anything against the God of Shadrach, Meshach and Abednego be cut into pieces and their houses be turned into piles of rubble, for no other god can save in this way."

Then the king promoted Shadrach, Meshach and Abednego in the province of Babylon.

Daniel 3:19-30 (NIV)

There are lessons we can learn from these young Hebrew boys in the manner of prayer that we are teaching in this book. Let me point out a few of these:

1) They were willing to risk their lives for their convictions.

All too often today our prayers are prayers of preference. In other words, when we are walking through our persuasion, and this process becomes too difficult, dangerous or unexpected, we change our prayers and our decisions for a less demanding route. We choose to relinquish what we would have achieved had we stayed the course, because of the difficulty of the passage. Convictions are beliefs we are willing to die for, persevere with and work through.

2) There are times that we have to defy legal laws in order to uphold moral laws.

It was immoral for Nebuchadnezzar to institute a law forcing everyone bow down to his golden idol when the music began to play. The three Hebrew boys however knew it was an immoral law. So, although it had been legislated, and it was now law to bow down to the golden idol, they made a decision to uphold moral law, which was to not worship anyone other than God. This meant they chose to defy the *legal* law. Now just to bring clarity here, I am not advocating breaking the law whenever a person feels the law is unjustified. There is a point in time though when the situation in a nation, or the place you have been positioned by God, is in dire need of God's intervention to save life, and to restore righteousness and truth. God has positioned every person strategically in life and the world, with a measure of His delegated authority to release His influence. Whether we use that authority or not is our choice. We need to speak into and take action in the domains in which God has placed us, thereby being agents of transformation with God. Now, if the church is as immoral as the society it is trying to reform, we have lost our voice, and we are no longer salt and light. This is where prescriptive prayer is so necessary.

A recent example of this is in Zimbabwe, where currently it is nearly impossible to obtain foreign exchange in banks, and the government says it is illegal to trade local money for foreign currency. This law has been made in the face of an economy which is not self-sustaining in any sector, and nothing can be brought into the country without using foreign currency to purchase it. If this law was to be blindly upheld the business sector would collapse, very little business actually functions in the country without the use of foreign currency. In fact, the government itself obtains foreign currency on the *black market*, known in Zimbabwe as the *parallel market*, purchasing foreign currency for their own projects. It is immoral to pass a law which the legislators do not even abide by, and that is actually unenforceable.

The knock-on effect of a blanket compliance with this legislation would rapidly cause businesses to collapse and liquidate, causing massive retrenchment of thousands of employees. As this is counterproductive economically and from the humanitarian aspect, it is preferable for businesses to stay viable, which they do against almost insurmountable odds. This is the dilemma we face. It is the principle that I am trying to teach that is important and regret that there is not time nor space to expand on the complexities here.

However, suffice it to say that it is immoral for a business person not to pay their staff. In order to do so though, they have to maintain viable businesses. In order to maintain a viable business, they cannot comply with the current legal law, but are forced to break the legal law. This is a catch-22 situation. Therefore I teach our congregation that if they get caught changing money they will have to suffer the consequences, which is usually a fine. However, that is a small price to pay if it means keeping the company going and their employees on the payroll, because in doing so they are able to bring in the necessary components to keep their businesses in existence.

In this case, defying the law because of its immoral nature makes perfect sense, and is necessary for survival and for righteousness. When we pray we must be willing to act in correspondence with our prayers.

3) The three young men were not afraid to answer the king.

Shadrach, Meshack and Abednigo's answer was the prescription to their dilemma. Listen carefully to their response:

Shadrach, Meshach and Abednego replied to the king, "O Nebuchadnezzar, we do not need to defend ourselves before you in this matter.

If we are thrown into the blazing furnace, the God we serve is able to save us from it, and he will rescue us from your hand, O king.

But even if he does not, we want you to know, O king, that we will not serve your gods or worship the image of gold you have set up."

Daniel 3:16-18

They never focused on the negative. They constantly affirmed what God could do and would do and what His Word had promised them. This kind of a prayer is surgical in nature. It draws the enemy into the cross-hairs of debate as to who is God. Nebuchadnezzar actually makes the statement, "What god can deliver you from my hand" (Daniel 3:15)? These young boys knew immediately when the issue of "who is God?" was raised, that their case was assured, just as with Elijah on Mount Carmel, "our God is a God who always answers by fire" (1 Kings 18:24).

Many Biblical scholars indicate that the verses dealing with these young boys' response are really both in the affirmative towards the king Nebuchadnezzar. These Hebrew boys left no room for doubt. They said to Nebuchadnezzar, "If we are thrown into the blazing furnace, the God we serve is able to save us from it, and he will rescue us from your hand, O king" (Daniel 3:17). This powerful affirmation declares their conviction and unwavering belief that God will save them from the king's hand and the fiery furnace.

But even if he does not, we want you to know, O king, that we will not serve your gods or worship the image of gold you have set up. Daniel 3:18 (NIV)

This verse almost sounds like a contradiction of their first affirmation, but this is where many scholars believe that the *he* really does not refer to God but to Nebuchadnezzar. What these young boys are saying is, "even if you don't throw us into the furnace we are not going to worship the image you set up." This kind of prayer seems more consistent with the character of God and the character of these young men.

For believers to get the same results we are going to have to pray and act with the same level of conviction.

4) When God answers, no one else can take the credit.

Everyone knows and everyone can see Who the fourth man in the fire is! This is truly reformation prayer.

"Then Nebuchadnezzar said, "Praise be to the God of Shadrach, Meshach and Abednego, who has sent his angel and rescued his servants! They trusted in him and defied the king's command and were willing to give up their lives rather than serve or worship any god except their own God.

Therefore I decree that the people of any nation or language who say anything against the God of Shadrach, Meshach and Abednego be cut into pieces and their houses be turned into piles of rubble, for no other god can save in this way."

Then the king promoted Shadrach, Meshach and Abednego in the province of Babylon.

Daniel 3:28-30 (NIV)

When our surgically accurate prayers are answered, everyone knows that it was God who answered them. These kinds of prayers can even turn the hearts of kings, let alone nations.

So often in the church and especially in prayer we want to prescribe solutions for situations that we don't understand. Often we hear from our pulpits preaching at problems. Most often this preaching simply delineates the problem and everyone shouts, *amen*! If we aren't preaching about the problems, we are often shouting at the institutions that we think should change and actually think that because we spoke to the issue, somehow the situation will change!

It is critically important for us to understand our role in initiating change in the world. We are not to be like the world and just criticize governments or factions or ideologies that we disagree with. We are to engage in the sphere or domain that God has placed us in, to be agents for change from within. For example, we have no record of Daniel or Joseph praying for the Government of their day to change, or for the authoritarian leaders to be removed. Instead both Daniel and Joseph received favor from God and were able to demonstrate the power of God's Kingdom by influential administration at the highest government level, in an ungodly situation. Both Daniel's and Joseph's prayers exalted the power of God and often changed the hearts of kings. This could not have happened however without their full engagement in the arenas in which they found themselves.

Prayers should be filled with prerequisites both for those praying as well as those for whom they are praying. For example a teacher who prays about a compromised value system, but is not willing to get involved and bring about change in that situation, renders their prayer ineffectual. One of the prerequisites that God places on prayer is that we should act in accordance with our prayer (Isaiah 58:1-14).

A banker praying about exorbitant interest rates, but not willing to get involved in changing the banking financial policy, is behaving irresponsibly and without understanding. God may move sovereignly to answer our prayers, but for the most part He uses people to bring about the answers. Certainly, for reformation to take place, we are all a part of the process.

Generational Prayer

The answers to prayer are often more complex than many prayer leaders want to admit or teach. Although God could sovereignly remove governments from power, to do so does not guarantee that God's leader would take the place of the former leader. We must understand that for certain situations prayers will only be answered generationally. This is particularly true when trying to remove principalities or powers that have been established in regions and continents over thousands of years. These kinds of strongholds will not be removed in a single prayer meeting, but for some, they will have to be removed by generations of prayer, since they have been established by generations of evil. We can, however, be assured, that whether in the short term or generationally, our prayers will be heard. Often in our *instant society* we expect instant answers to our prayers. I frequently think of prayers that were only answered long after the saints who prayed them have died. These testimonies speak of trans-generational praying, that for many of us has almost become a lost art. God is trying to get His Church to stretch itself beyond the comfort zones it often creates for itself.

Agency–Angels

As we study this attribute of surgical prayer it is important that we understand the agency through which many of our prayers are answered or helped. God desires the church to be engaged in supernatural activity. One of the primary agencies God uses is angels. In the gospel of Luke we see Jesus in the Garden of Gethsemane, "He withdrew about a stone's throw beyond them, knelt down and prayed, "Father, if you are willing, take this cup from me; yet not my will, but yours be done" (Luke 22:41-44). An angel from heaven appeared to him and strengthened him. And being in anguish, he prayed more earnestly, and his sweat was like drops of blood falling to the ground."

Jesus is assisted by an angel while he was praying. It is important to understand this assistance comes only after he had begun to pray. Angels often come to assist you and help you to pray earnestly. We don't fully know the benefits of angels. We do know, however that, angels have engaged in assisting men and are recorded as doing so throughout Scripture. In fact Hebrews 1:7 "In speaking of the angels he says, "He makes his angels winds, his servants flames of fire." And again, "Are not all angels ministering spirits sent to serve those who will inherit salvation" (Hebrews 1:14). Although believers do not command angels, nor do we know entirely the extent of their operation and assistance, we do know that angels respond to prayers.

In Ecclesiastes we see this relationship between the words of men and the activity of angels:

> **"Do not be rash with your mouth, And let not your heart utter anything hastily before God. For God is in heaven, and you on earth; Therefore let your words be few.**
>
> **When you make a vow to God, do not delay to pay it; For He has no pleasure in fools. Pay what you have vowed—**
>
> **Better not to vow than to vow and not pay.**
>
> **Do not let your mouth cause your flesh to sin, nor say before the messenger of God [angel] that it was an error. Why should God be angry at your excuse and destroy the work of your hands?"**
>
> **Ecclesiastes 5:2,4-6 (NKJV)**

This verse seems to indicate that our mouths can hinder the work of angels in our lives and in fact we can tear down what we have built up by sinning with our mouth before our angel.

Perseverance is a Force

Prescriptive surgical prayer requires patience. Every time you see the word patience I suggest that you replace it with the word perseverance. Perseverance is a force that works on our behalf, especially in prayer. We read in Hebrews that,

You need to persevere so that when you have done the will of God, you will receive what he has promised.

For in just a very little while, "He who is coming will come and will not delay.

But my righteous one will live by faith. And if he shrinks back, I will not be pleased with him.

But we are not of those who shrink back and are destroyed, but of those who believe and are saved."

Hebrews 10:36-39 (NIV)

We all have need of perseverance so that after you have prayed the will of God you might receive the promise. In our world today we know very little of persevering in prayer. This is part of the prescription for successful prayer. When I think of perseverance that brings about reformation I often think of people like Pat Robertson and other Christian leaders in the United States, that began to tackle issues through the court system. These leaders encouraged activism and called the church to corporate prayer, and today the courts have seen and continue to see major adjustments. Because these men not only prayed, but were willing to follow their prayers with sustained action, they have preserved a measure of godly rule for another generation.

Some people have come and prophesied that Zimbabwe will become the Switzerland of Africa. It may happen, but I don't believe it will happen because of prayer or prophecy only. It will happen over a period of time as people pray, get involved, get the skills and learn how to lead and govern.

Rees Howell in his book *Intercessor* speaks of the historical difference prayer may have made during World War II. I highly recommend that you read his book because this is the kind of influence that it will take to bring about a modern day reformation.

Fredrick Chiluba, ex-Zambian President, declared his nation a Christian nation after he was installed as president. He was instrumental in bringing about some very good changes to his country, and yet after two terms in office, he tried to violate his own law on term limits. He admitted that the power of politics had so affected him that he had lost sight of his original intentions. He became embroiled in controversy and scandal as he was accused of corruption.

Easy to Obtain, Hard to Maintain!

One of the lessons that we have learned is that it is easy to obtain things, but hard to maintain. If we're going to maintain what we have advanced in prayer, we're going to have to work hard at prescribing frameworks and holding ourselves accountable to them. It is easy to pray, but challenging to act practically and in line with reformation on what we've prayed. I believe that it is important to begin to hold ourselves accountable about what we pray and prophesy.

There have been many prayers and prophecies declared in Zimbabwe by leaders from around the world, many of whom are prominent. One in particular declared, "I see someone dying in office, but I don't see anyone dying from farm takeovers." Instead, no one died in office and forty people died from violent farm takeovers. This leader's prophecy had received wide cir- culation throughout Zimbabwe, based on their earlier prophesy, which had been well-received by the nation. The credibility of this leader, as well as the credibility of prophecy and prophetic prayer suffered greatly because there was no accountability by the prophet.

Agency—Man

When leaders prophesy or pray corporately over nations or situations without a proper framework and an appropriate prescription, there is a tendency, especially in some circles, to begin to exaggerate and overstate what God is going to do, and so raise false expectations. The fact of the matter is, that just because it is prophesied or prayed doesn't mean God is obligated to bring it to pass. Although God can and does answer in Sovereign ways, as He did when He spoke to Mary telling her that she would bear Jesus, the agency that God most often uses on earth is man.

Many people do not understand that God is Spirit and as such is limited by His word and nature to spiritual activity. God needs yielded flesh through which He can operate on earth. I believe that we have limited what God has wanted to do on earth by our unavailability or unwillingness to follow His prompting. It is evident from what Jesus says, that, "unless we do the will of the Father who is in heaven, we cannot enter the kingdom of heaven" (Matthew 7:21). How can God use us to extend His kingdom on earth, if through disobedience we refuse to enter in? "These are hard words" (John 6:60), to coin a phrase! Therefore in soberness we accept that little is going to happen here on earth, without God using a man to bring it to pass. God used Adam, and Noah, He used Abraham, Isaac, Jacob and Joseph, Moses and Joshua and so the list goes on. Cover to cover the Bible records men used by God to carry out His purpose and His will here on earth. To this He has called us, will we follow (Luke 9:23)? The agency that God uses to bring about reformation on earth is man, filled with His spirit. Man must engage in follow-through for prayers prayed and prophecies given. That is what Paul meant when he said to

Timothy that he must, "war according to the prophecies that were spoken over his life" (1 Timothy 1:18,19). This is prescriptive prayer. Using prophecy, affirmations and prayer with corresponding action to accomplish God's will on earth.

Testimony: Jeff Mzwimbi

One of Business Domain leaders, Pastor Jeff Mzwimbi, has fought giants and known first hand the deliverance of God, as most in the body of Christ have not. His life mirrors that of King David, or Joseph, or Moses. A man with a clear and powerful call of God on his life. Early on in his Christian walk he saw miracles, the favor of God, but like these three giants in the faith, has faced his bears and lions and Goliaths. He initially worked closely with Strive Masiyiwa in the establishing and running of Econet Wireless Network a cellular service provider built and established by believers in Zimbabwe. Later he started and headed up one of the first indigenous banks in our nation, but like Joseph was put through unjust imprisonment, lengthy court battles and, like Moses and Job, had lost all that he had built up. At this point in his remarkable story, the courts have ruled him innocent. He has known all along and can see now, this has all been a part of a process of reformation that he is heading up and which continues to this day.

Jeff shares with us:

The subject of prayer is a matter close to my heart and I view myself as a student of prayer, taking up early classes in the school of prayer. I enrolled in this school when the Econet battle started in 1995. A bit of background information is worth mentioning here. Econet Wireless was a God-inspired company, founded and headed by Strive Masiyiwa. Before any mention of cell phones in Zimbabwe was made, Strive got the vision and the equipment for this venture. As with many success stories, he faced severe persecution from the powers that be in our nation, who not only refused his application for a license to run a cellular phone network, but they also set up their own cell phone company and took Strives equipment.

The company won its application for a license after four and a half years worth of court battles, at one point Strive himself even having to face five supreme court judges alone. At the beginning of the Econet battle, I was partnered with Strive. For the next several years I learned the power of prayer in the marketplace. Most importantly I learned that without prayer my success as a Christian businessman would be short-lived.

Early in the Econet battle, I discovered that we do not fight against flesh and blood, but principalities and powers in heavenly places. Each time we descend to the level of the natural realm we find ourselves ill-equipped to wage war. Our opponents at that level are in full amour to which we have no access. Our weapons are spiritual. In the early days I took comfort in an understanding that I since have discovered was in error. I thought that when I waged spiritual warfare, my opponents were unarmed and therefore I had full reign in the realm of the spirit. It took me quite some time to realize that the enemy also operates in the spirit realm and that my assumptions were incorrect.

I have since discovered that the battleground of the spirit realm is drenched in blood. On the enemy side, it is full of the blood of bulls, goats, chickens, wild animals and even human beings. On our side, it is covered by the powerful saving blood of Jesus. The enemy understands sacrifice and uses it to move powers of darkness in his favor. By manipulating the realm of the supernatural, he moves forces of fortune and favor in his direction, as long as there are no counter-forces from the Christian businessmen. I believe that the dark forces are evoked more in the realm of business than in any other sphere.

For many years we had prayed fervently, fasted more than we ate, read the word regularly, and attended every church service and every prayer meeting without fail. Yet to us the enemy still appeared invincible on the outside. Court rulings were against us, we lost the tender process and every attempt to negotiate failed dismally. Some of the Christian brothers urged us to give up and try something else. In all this, however, there was an unusual, serene spirit over us, and an inner confidence that all would be well, and the ever present voice of our man of God encouraging us to possess the land.

When the Econet battle was finally won, we had been to the High Court four times and the Supreme Court once. In between we witnessed unusual divine incidences. Finance to keep the company going for four years without revenues was the most outstanding miracle. Just keeping the qualified staff on board was another miracle in itself. When the cellular license was sent for tender, and the opposing company Telecel judged the winner, it appeared like the end of the road for us. Only to find a few days later, that all eight adjudicators had made a simple arithmetic error in calculations! This opened the process to a court challenge! It was winning this court challenge that finally succeeded in the cellular license being awarded to Econet.

In all that period I learned a lot about prayer. I learned that God's purposes cannot be frustrated by man, no matter who that man is and how powerful he might be. God's purposes will prevail. Many things were spoken by a number of people during that time. I also learned that there were many 'prophetic' voices speaking to us all the time. It was critical however to know which voice to listen to, and which to disregard!

I also learned the importance of combining prayer with giving. In the circumstances we were in, giving was painful because I had "nothing" to give. Yet I still desired to give even the little I had. I gave without "knowledge." At that stage of my Christian walk I did not understand the powerful impact of giving in the spiritual realm. So I gave, not with the understanding to provoke the supernatural, but in some cases to simply feel good about myself, by meeting a need in the ministry and in others. Even though I did not fully understand it, my giving resulted in me receiving blessings and rewards. Every gift, I learned, had its blessing. I discovered that it was more blessed to give than to receive. It did not however break into the realm that I was seeking to break into.

It was not until I decided to get seriously involved in building the Celebration Centre that I entered a new realm in my prayer life. There was a desire, a hunger and a thirst for God that came with involving my finances in the things of God at a deeper level. The more I gave, the more I wanted to pray. The more I enjoyed prayer, the more I experienced fulfillment in the spirit. I just could not be left out in the things of the spirit. I sensed almost tangible spiritual growth and felt very comfortable in the house of God doing the things of God. I think I caught a glimpse of how Solomon felt after a thousand burnt offerings, when God asked him what he wanted, and then he later went on to give ten thousand burnt offerings. God's response to Solomon's prayer at the dedication of the temple is one of the finest scriptures in the Old Testament and in the history of the Jewish people.

I realized that Solomon gave so that his prayers could be answered. He went on to be the richest man in the world, who managed his wealth with a business acumen no one had ever achieved before, and no one has achieved after him. I believe Solomon knew the odds against him becoming a king, given the way he had entered the palace. To deal with the forces against him he needed to provoke the supernatural, and simple prayers would not do it. He gave beyond what anybody had ever done and his prayers could not be ignored in the supernatural realm. For me this was by far the most important lesson of all.

By this time I had begun to realize that prayer had to be accompanied by giving. These two actions had a connection that had a divine pattern and principle. I saw that giving was like wrapping paper around prayer that was being sent to heaven. Poor wrapping paper devalued the gift inside and spoke volumes about what the giver thought of the recipient. Costly wrapping paper spoke volumes about the person giving and how they valued the recipient and the gift inside. I realized that our prayers are like that. Sometimes we had sent our prayers "unwrapped" and it was no wonder that no matter how "powerful" they may have seemed as prayers, because they were cheaply presented before the Lord of Hosts, they had little effect! Cornelius was a fine example in the New Testament of the recognition in the Heavens of gifts and prayer going hand in hand to provoke a supernatural response (Acts 10:1-48).

The level of giving (wrapping) I now understood had to be high in order for it to stand out. The gift did not need to be high in terms of monetary value, but it did need to be high in what it cost me the giver. This was sacrifice. As Pastor Tom said, "until the level of our sacrifice exceeds that of our forefathers' sacrifice to demons we will miss the mark — never turn the tide in our nation."

As a businessman I had come to realize that the marketplace had intense spiritual activity competing for wealth and power. When anyone entered that realm desirous to be a serious player and make an impact for the kingdom, they had to be equipped to do battle and possess what God had given them. Prayer and giving therefore became formidable weapons.

A paradox I increasingly experienced, was that although God had given us the land to possess, the land was occupied, even though it was ours by right. Although we had been given it, we did not possess it in practice. So, we did not possess what was ours! This initially seemed contradictory, but I was learning that to possess anything in the natural, I first had to take possession of it in the spiritual. Paul said, "we have been blessed with every spiritual blessing in the heavenly places in Christ" (Ephesians 1:3). On God's side there is no more work to be done. It was all done by Christ, and our entitlement to the land was sealed for us to possess, but this was in the spirit not in the natural. It was in the supernatural realm that we have been blessed with all spiritual blessing and not in the natural realm. I had to learn how to activate what was waiting for us in the spirit, and that was through prayer and giving. My natural abilities would not take me to where God had set aside for me to be. I encountered natural resistance caused by man and in some cases greater than I could handle. In most cases the natural resistance was beyond my capabilities. I needed supernatural intervention to cause things to move in my favor. A prayer for such intervention that had no sacrificial giving could only have a measure of success, and would not deal the enemy a decisive blow.

When Joshua led the children of Israel for the conquest of Canaan land which was given to them but not possessed, Jericho became the sacrifice. Once Jericho was given as first fruits to God, supernatural help came to Joshua to defeat the kings of the land. The sun and the moon even stood still for Joshua, so that he could defeat five kings! Later on he defeated 27 kings with an army that was trained on the job! It was supernatural help to take natural land, after the entire booty of the first supernatural victory had been sacrificed to God.

Pastor's message on, "How long will you neglect to go and possess the land which the Lord God of your fathers has given to you" (Joshua 18:3), challenged me to the core. I realized that the burden was on us, not on God, to take the land. God had already given us the land. Neglect here referred to slackness, and this slackness was both in giving and in prayer. When I've been slack in these two areas, I've been unable to possess the land, because my trust was in my natural abilities and these tell me of every giant in the land. When I give and pray at a serious level, I have supernatural help and the giants disappear.

I believe now is the time for us to turn from slackness and begin to move into the land through prayer and giving supernatural help and the giants disappear.

Chapter 7
Surgical Prayer is Prophetic

There has been a great revival of the prophetic in the Church. As we move into a greater understanding of the role of the prophetic in the Church we are seeing it permeate every aspect of the life of the Church. This is especially true in the realm of prayer, and is particularly effective in helping prayer become surgically accurate.

By definition *prophecy* means: "foretelling of future events, inspired or prophetic utterances, public interpretation of Scripture" (Chambers English Dictionary).

Jesus tells His disciples that, "when the Spirit of truth, has come, He will guide you into all truth; for He will not speak on His own authority, but whatever He hears He will speak; and He will tell you things to come" (John 16:13 NKJV). Evidence of this in the early Church is seen, "when Paul had laid hands on them, the Holy Spirit came upon them, and they spoke with tongues and *prophesied*" (Acts 19:6 NKJV). As Paul says, "Now we have received, not the spirit of the world, but the Spirit who is from God, that we might know the things that have been freely given to us by God" (1 Corinthians 2:12 NKJV). He also says, "we have the mind of Christ" (1 Corinthians 2:16 NIV). So we know that today we can all function prophetically through the power of the Holy Spirit, we can all pray surgically using *prophetic prayer*.

The Creative Power of The Spoken Word

Prophecy comes from the mind of God, but through the mouth of man, therefore we need to be available to God for Him to speak through us.

The Lord says, "So shall My Word be that goes forth from My mouth; It shall not return to Me void, But it shall accomplish what I please, And it shall prosper in the thing for which I sent it." Isaiah 55:11

The creative power of the Word of God released into the earth, which was "without form, and void", caused the light to come, the structure was formed and life created and multiplied. It was a powerful, word-based event (Genesis 1:1-3 NIV). Our situations may be just like that, "without form and void, and in darkness," but because we have been made in the image and likeness of God, we too can release God's creative Word into those dark places, and see the power of His Word bring light, structure and life. Although mankind has fallen from the position God originally intended for him, the Lord Jesus reconciled us back to God and to our rightful place of dominion. In the early 1970's a charismatic leader declared that, "God's Word in our mouths is as powerful as God's Word in His mouth." So we should take up this awesome privilege and begin behaving like the children of God, and be about our Father's business, extending His influence wherever we go. We must remember though after we have spoken out these prophetic prayers, to guard our mouths, so that in our conversation we do not negate our prayers with negative predictions. These would amount to negative declarations and talk, leading to the eventual destruction of the very things we are trying to build!

In the Old Testament, prophets were called *seers*. Today the body of Christ still needs seers who can responsibly lead domain prayer, constantly keeping in touch with their prophetic insight. In many of our prayer meetings, the corporate group's awareness of the constant guidance from the Holy Spirit needs to increase. The appropriate framework in which prophetic prayer should function must also be set in place. This is applied through establishment of the appropriate authority structure, which includes clear accountability. This manner of praying can bring about transformation and reformation like no other. The Bible teaches us that, "...everyone who prophesies speaks to men for their strengthening, encouragement and comfort" (1 Corinthians 14:3). Prophetic prayer follows the same pattern, so its effect can be very dynamic.

Paul is the perfect New Testament example of this type of prayer. Although an apostle and a teacher, Paul also walked under a strong prophetic anointing. This was revealed as a profound, revelatory gift, for uncovering and explaining the large corporate purpose of the Church. Paul himself says, "I wish that you all spoke in tongues, but even more that you would prophesy; and greater is one who prophesies than one who speaks in tongues (1 Corinthians 14:5)."

It is imperative that the Church once again begins to apply the prophetic in not only speaking about and preaching about the Kingdom, but in demonstrating the Kingdom. Jesus says, "Let your light so shine before men, that they may *see your good works* and glorify your Father in heaven" (Matthew 5:16 NKJV). Notice, He does not say *hear your good words!* This demonstration of the Kingdom in life, is a responsibility that begins with individual believers, our families, proceeding from the

local church thus extending our influence in the community, the society at large and the nation in which we have
been placed. We must remember that all change starts
from the inside out, one person at a time. Once an individual begins to operate in the prophetic he can affect his
family and they can be prophetic also. A prophetic family can impact a church. A prophetic church can impact
a city. A city that's been influenced can change a nation.
Once nations are transformed and reformed they can
bring influence to bear on the world.

Prophetic Prayer and
Social Responsibility

For the church to appear to be prophetic to the
world, it must make the invisible visible, and the visible
must be understood. "Let your light so shine before
men, that they may see your good works and glorify your
Father in heaven" (Matthew 5:16 NKJV). It is evident
from this Scripture that what we do will be seen by men,
and there will be a resultant change in the way they see
God. This will exert influence in the world for the
Kingdom.

Jesus' emphasis is always towards tangible results.
When He, "sent his servants to the tenants to collect His
fruit," the tenants killed the servants and His son. What is
our response when He sends His servants to us to collect
His fruit? We should not take lightly Jesus' reprimand to
the Pharisees, "Therefore I tell you that the kingdom of
God will be taken away from you and given to a people
who will produce its fruit" (Matthew 21:43 NIV).

A few of the practical things that we have done
which have proven to be prophetic, have to do with being
a voice of reformation in the specific domains in which
God has placed us.

Inception of Compassion Ministries

One of my earliest experiences of this was in 1984, a couple of years after we had started the church. I was taken by a member of our congregation to a bus stop on the outskirts of a nearby city, and shown 200 people that had been displaced because of the war in Mozambique. As I looked upon the malnourished and dying women and children my heart broke. I went back to our fledgling congregation and painted a prophetic vision of what we could do to help. It took us two weeks to gather seven tons of food and clothing and to purchase a 10 ton truck to haul everything. Our band of volunteers set out with Quioxtic zeal, which vaporized instantly in dismay and horror on our arrival at the bus stop, now overrun by more than 2,000 refugees! What ensued was hardly prophetic as we were mobbed and ran for our lives. The people flogged and beat each other in their desperate attempts to secure food and clothing for themselves and their children. Two hours later, after the ruckus had died down, we sneaked back to the truck with our tails between our legs. I stared in stony silence, numbly gathering my shattered emotions and jumbled impressions, reeling from what I had just witnessed and experienced. In vain I attempted to marshal my thoughts into some sort of order, for a report back to the congregation of our first refugee outreach trip; perplexed at how our best intentions and well thought-out plans had gone so radically awry.

Not to be deterred after this traumatic initiation, we pushed through to begin an adventure that continues to this day. Within six months of our shattering failure, a major donor had given us 160 tons of rice. This we were able to exchange with the national Grain Marketing Board at a rate of 3:1 for mealie meal, the staple diet of the local people in the region. Overnight we became the largest distributor of food in the nation. The food-relief side of our operation was short-lived, as the United Nations and other world donors came on the scene. We shifted our efforts to clothing relief and to "meeting people's needs, spirit, soul and body," the Mission Statement of Compassion Ministries. The effect of our early intervention was that we were able to have our evangelists in every refugee camp at a time when no other churches were allowed permanent ministry leaders in the camps. This led to the establishment of great churches inside the camps, as we were able to lead 65,000 of the 144,000 refugees to Jesus. Ten years later 38,000 were members of our church, and when they were repatriated to Mozambique, they established churches throughout each of the provinces from which they had fled. Today we keep in touch with these churches which are still growing and have become a beachhead for our message of reformation to the nation of Mozambique.

Testimony: Winnie Kanoyangwa

Just like the story of Mozambique, we have endeavored to put prophetic prayers into practice in every domain. In the sphere of prison ministry we see this applied in the life of Winnie Kanoyangwa. She and her husband were forced to walk through a land mine field as human shields, by white Rhodesian forces, in order to clear their way. She lost her husband as well as her own right eye, right arm and right knee cap. When she found Jesus, she chose to forgive those who had caused her such pain, and turned her shattered life towards the lives of those in hospital and in prison. Winnie spends her days pouring out love, attention and care on everyone she meets. Her life is truly prophetic in the domains in which she is positioned.

Victory Business Forum, Celebration Holdings International and Gatekeepers

Our leading business people have banded together and created a forum to discuss and dialogue about reformation in the market place. We call this the Victory Business Forum (VBF). The entire aim of this Forum is to equip the business leaders of today and tomorrow with kingdom principles and patterns for reformation of their called domain. From this dynamic group of leaders has been birthed the engine room that provides provision for the ever expanding work of the ministry vision. Out of the need to manage the gifts and donations in cash, share certificates and in kind generated by the members of the church and through VBF we have raised up a wing of the ministry that we call *Celebration Holdings International* (CHI). Celebration Holdings is the profit wing of the ministry and is determined to endow all aspects of the ministry, by harnessing the power of dedicated Kingdom business people, and creating a structure for them to work within.

We are creating structures financially that allow people not only to give, but to invest their finances in such a way so as to bring good returns on their investments as well as funding the ministry. In fact, a recent development of this is that many of our domain prayer people have begun to emerge as Gatekeepers. Gatekeepers are those who control the flow of people, ideas and resources in and out of the gate of the domains that they have taken responsibility for in prayer and practice.

This means that if the Television Department needs a piece of new equipment, there is already a team of people committed to providing for that requirement. In this way their prayers not only speak to the problem, but their actions are the answer to the problem. This is truly prophetic surgical prayer.

Education

Education is one of the most powerful and formative aspects of a nation's life. We saw the vital necessity to bring reformation into this critical area as it directly influences the lives of the future leaders of the nation, either positively or negatively. Tertiary education is the level at which leaders of the nation are impacted and influenced. The need to represent a Biblical world view is probably more prophetic and necessary today than at any other time in history. In the face of what many call the *post-Christian era*, the need for the Church to reform itself and its approach to society has never been greater. Celebration College has established schools in five disciplines namely: Business, Medical, Education, Ministry and Music, Dance and Arts. We teach in these five domains from a strong biblical and principled foundation, which we believe acts as a prophetic voice into the nation.

Entertainment

The idea of reformation has even spilled over into the vision of the Business leaders of our community. Recently the leading advertising agency in our city, hosted an *Idols* competition in our nation. Throughout the 13 weeks leading up to the night of the final competition, the host and owner of the agency, who is a strong member of the church, interlaced the entire program with solid prophetic reformation pieces. Calling the nation to uphold positive values and sound morals, emphasized by showcasing young people with rags to riches stories. These were powerful testimonies of how both their personal lives, as well as their artistic creativity and performance had been touched by God. Overall the evening saw musical talent discovered and rewarded in an atmosphere of stiff competition, but in an overarching way the Good News was spread from one of the highest profile programs in Zimbabwe with peak viewership.

The final program was televised and played out on the stage of our very own Celebration Centre Facility. The church's television crew taped the program for national viewing. The sold-out audience was treated to a state-of-the-art facility and program, and throughout the program frequent mention was made of the Church's role and support, God's intervention and the promoter's faith. In a nation where millions have fled and the economy is in hyper-inflation and most businesses are either in retreat or hibernation, this businessman stepped out prophetically and really made a difference. He touched the whole nation with entertainment interwoven with the message of hope and reformation. This kind of activity is domain prayer in action. Oh, and did I mention that the owner of this business is one of the prayer domain leaders in the Media, Entertainment and Sports Prayer Domain?!

Television Ministry

Early in the ministry I felt that God wanted me to advance our ministry through television. Many prophecies were spoken over our lives about broadcasting our message around the world. A number of my friends were doing television and made it look so easy. I was able to secure some second-hand equipment and began taping rudimentary teachings and interviews, but with no real focus. We began to raise up a team of people to help us put programs together, but before we could launch our first program they all took their new-learned skills and went to work in the secular market place. This was very discouraging and yet I felt compelled to persevere with pursuit of this dream, both by the desire to reach multitudes of people, and by the prophetic words that so often came to me.

Although our initial attempt had crashed and burned, eight years later it was resurrected when I purchased an excellent second-hand professional television production suite. Once again we were able to gather many skilled technicians, and after releasing a few programs, the temptation for them to use their skills in the market place was too great. Once again I saw them scatter, this time to the United Kingdom and Australia to ply their new-found skills. I must admit that when the second group of television production technicians and film crew left I felt crushed. I almost despaired of doing television out of third world Africa. Nevertheless the prophetic kept prompting me to pursue the dream.

In 2003 we moved into our new sanctuary, a prophetic structure, where I had applied visionary planning by having all the underground trunking and cables necessary for television laid. It was two years later, 2005, that I was invited to begin to air a program on the Loveworld Christian Network that beamed throughout Africa, the Middle East, parts of Europe, Asia and Australia. We started producing our programs with the lowest range of professional equipment we could find. This time we had turned a corner. With daily prayer now established and strongly praying into the television ministry and those involved in the television ministry fully given to the vision, the programs were a success and there was marked growth of the TV Ministry. We soon built a state of the art production studio, with the best brand new equipment. Unlike the two previous attempts, this time the crew and staff were totally unqualified and cut their teeth working with us in the ministry, and although their skills are now constantly being head-hunted by the corporate world, their loyalty to vision, their sense of calling and their obedience to the prophetic call, is helping us to produce an excellent program that is touching millions of lives. "Though the vision tarry, wait for it, for it shall surely come to pass" (Habakkuk 2:3 NKJV).

We had experienced Psalm 126:6 first hand, "He who goes to and fro weeping, carrying his bag of seed, Shall indeed come again with a shout of joy, bringing his sheaves with him." As well as Psalm 30:5 "Weeping may last for the night, But a shout of joy comes in the morning."

Prophetic praying and expectation is common throughout the Scriptures, for example, Anna in the book of Matthew was found in the temple praying about the coming Messiah.

There was also a prophetess, Anna, the daughter of Phanuel, of the tribe of Asher. She was very old; she had lived with her husband seven years after her marriage,

and then was a widow until she was eighty-four. She never left the temple but worshipped night and day, fasting and praying.

Coming up to them at that very moment, she gave thanks to God and spoke about the child to all who were looking forward to the redemption of Jerusalem.
Luke 2:36-38 (NIV)

Notice that Anna "spoke about the child to all who were looking forward to the redemption of Jerusalem." Speaking out or affirming to people of like-mind amplifies the power of the prophetic.

She also had a strong prophetic spirit to endure in prayer before the Lord, even when much time went by where nothing seemed to be happening. The anointing for prophetic intercession always imparts the grace for endurance. This is something that my wife and I have experienced first hand in our ministry in Africa. We have been sustained here over the period of more than 25 years of ministry, against all odds, because of this powerful impartation of grace.

Moved by the Spirit

Again in the same Scripture we see Simeon, a man who had the Holy Spirit on him, and probably knew Anna, as he too was "waiting for the consolation of Israel." Unity of spirit and a common purpose in the prophetic, again amplifies the power of the spoken-out Word of God.

Now there was a man in Jerusalem called Simeon, who was righteous and devout. He was waiting for the consolation of Israel, and the Holy Spirit was upon him.

It had been revealed to him by the Holy Spirit that he would not die before he had seen the Lord's Christ.

***Moved by the Spirit*, he went into the temple courts. When the parents brought in the child Jesus to do for him what the custom of the Law required,**

Simeon took him in his arms and praised God, saying:

"Sovereign Lord, as you have promised, you now dismiss your servant in peace.

For my eyes have seen your salvation,

which you have prepared in the sight of all people,

a light for revelation to the Gentiles and for glory to your people Israel."

The child's father and mother marvelled at what was said about him.

Then Simeon blessed them and said to Mary, his mother: "This child is destined to cause the falling and rising of many in Israel, and to be a sign that will be spoken against,

so that the thoughts of many hearts will be revealed. And a sword will pierce your own soul too."

Luke 2:25-35 (NIV)

Do you notice here that Simeon was, "Moved by the Spirit" so he went into the temple courts at just the time that Joseph and Mary brought Jesus there. There is such a difference between praying what you want to happen, and praying according to the will of God. Both Simeon and Anna wanted to see the redemption of Israel, but they were both tuned-in to the Spirit, moved by Him and persevered until they received the breakthrough of the promise God had given them both.

Projection

Neither Anna nor Simeon tried to modify what God had given them to do, they were faithful to His Word to them. Altering the specific known Word that God has assigned us to pray about and to take action on, is called projection. This is one of the greatest hindrances in ministry. When we allow our own opinions, desires, and wishful thinking, none of which is the mind of Christ, to start coloring and changing the known Word of God to us, we are modifying and qualifying what we pray and say. Simeon and Anna had no personal agenda, they would receive no direct personal gain from their prophetic voice, other than the joy of fulfilling the mandate of God. They did it to serve God, to respond to God in the context of prayer and fasting. So in this context, "Let us fix our eyes on Jesus, the author and perfecter of our faith, who for the joy set before Him endured the cross, scorning its shame, and sat down at the right hand of the throne of God" (Hebrews 12:2 NIV). It is also interesting to note that, like Jesus, neither Anna nor Simeon were part of the established leadership of the day.

Please don't get offended with these observations, nor fearful about prophetic prayer. I'm just suggesting we revisit these issues and the techniques that have become commonplace in corporate prayer, and which diminish its impact. I believe in prayer, in healing, in prophecy and the gifts of the Spirit. I want to see effective prayer and prophecy functioning in the Church and in our lives. For the Kingdom to expand, prayer must be spiritual and not the works of fleshly man. It must be in the power of the Spirit just as it was with Jesus, Simeon and Anna. What we've begun in the spirit cannot be completed in the flesh (Galatians 3:3 NIV).

Protocol for Prophetic Prayer

One very significant factor we need to appreciate and understand is God's provision and protocol to accomplish prophetic prayer in the corporate setting. God has set pastors to direct and initiate the process of prophetic prayer. God has appointed pastors to lead the local church and equips them with His vision for each local church. God has assigned anyone planted as members in those churches to carry out that vision. Communication of vision from the pastor to the designated prayer domain leaders is critical. Effective transfer of the mandate will directly impact the results that are seen from churches' corporate prayer meetings. Corporate prayer meetings are often "destroyed for a lack of knowledge" (Hosea 4:6 KJV), or conversely established by the effective, maintained communication of the vision. It is essential for us to understand that it is easier to obtain the vision from God, than it is to maintain it, both for leaders and for the people they serve. As the body constantly needs air to live, as it needs blood continuously to function, people need vision continually to stay alive spiritually (Hosea 4:6), and to actively establish the purpose of God. When the man of God speaks, and we heed the Word of God in his mouth, the Scripture says we will prosper.

Believe in the LORD your God, and you shall be established; believe His prophets, and you will succeed.
2 Chronicles 20:20 (NKJV)

Testimony: Tinotenda Chanakira

Tinotenda Chanakira is a young man with great vision, but who was struggling to progress and was disconnected from the Lord, from the vision and the visionary, the man of God, that would release what he needed to accomplish his vision.

Tinotenda's mother tells his story:

We asked Pastor Tom's oldest son, Tommy Deuschle, to pray for our son Tinotenda in July, 2006 when he was home on vacation. Tinotenda had been playing tennis since he was six, and had been in California, USA for one and a half years. His tennis had not improved dramatically and we were struggling to finance his career. As parents we also had communication problems with our son and he would sulk a lot and preferred to be on his own, locked up in his room. Tommy prayed for him and prophesied into his life.

We were overawed at the amazing events which took place after Tommy had prayed and prophesied over Tinotenda. Just as when Samuel prophesied over Saul that, "the Spirit of the LORD will come upon you, and you will prophesy with them and be turned into another man.

"And let it be, when these signs come to you, that you do as the occasion demands; for God is with you" (1 Samuel 10:6,7).

Tinotenda traveled to Holland where he won two tournaments. This was a record achievement.

Tinotenda has taken part on several ITF Futures tennis tournaments where he has excelled.

His game has improved tremendously and he has attracted the attention of some top international coaches.

We have managed to raise finance for him to travel round the world to practice and play tournaments in preparation for him to turn professional.

Since then our relationship has improved greatly. We talk a lot and he is very open and extremely cooperative. He appreciates what we are doing for him.

We believe that the prophetic prayer by Tommy broke some bondages that were holding back our son and his tennis career. We believe that our son will compete at Wimbledon, will win several grand slams and masters. We believe the prayer by Tommy opened a very successful and prosperous tennis career. It opened doors, which no man can close. We believe that Tinotenda is going to achieve in tennis what no other man has ever achieved in tennis from Zimbabwe. We believe that a when a prophet or man of God speaks into one's life, the life of that person will never be the same. Tommy spoke into Tinotenda's life and Tinotenda will never be the same.

Chapter 8
Surgical Prayer is Pastoral

The term *pastor* is used only once in the King James version of the Bible, and is found in Ephesians 4:11,12 NIV, "It was he who gave some to be apostles, some to be prophets, some to be evangelists, and some to be pastors and teachers, to prepare God's people for works of service, so that the body of Christ may be built up." It is derived from the Greek word *poimen*, which means *a shepherd* or *pastor*, and is primarily translated as *shepherd* throughout the New Testament. That the word *pastor* is only used once in the New Testament seems strange, when the office is the most widely recognized in the Church today. However there are a number of additional references which use similar words, primarily *shepherd* as well as terms such as overseer, elder and apostle. It is God who calls and equips people to shepherd and pastor his flock. The greatest example of a pastor was the Great Shepherd, Jesus, who, "...when he saw the multitudes...was moved with compassion for them, because they fainted, and were scattered abroad, as sheep having no shepherd" (Matthew 9:36).

As we have seen there are a variety of terms which have been translated to describe the person appointed by God to shepherd His people. These terms depict a function and not a position or hierarchy in the church. They all simply indicate the person appointed by God to have oversight for the flock in a particular location. In this capacity the shepherd is the one appointed by God to lead. He does not, therefore, wake up and consult the chief sheep! The pastor is the leader, the one with the responsibility given him by God for the local church. He has the mantle and the vision for that church, and he is the one mandated to direct the prayer in the church. If the pastor is not willing to take responsibility for prayer, there can be no surgical prayer. If there is no pastor or shepherd in prayer, then prayer will be scattered, just as the sheep are scattered when there is no shepherd. People will gather to pray, but with no leader, each will pray according to their own desires and agendas. The local and national church corporate cannot operate in power with an individual, independent type of prayer. There must be a pastor, a shepherd, directing the flock in prayer, in order to achieve surgical prayer for that flock, and so to see the power of God released in that region.

Before prayer can be effective, two things must happen:

Firstly, the pastor of the church must have a vision and secondly he must be engaged in guiding, directing and overseeing prayer. The pastor is the head overseer of the local flock; the flock is under his headship and governance. Prayer without governance leads to confusion, deception, even manipulation. We have all been in or heard of meetings commandeered by intercessory zealots. This is not to denigrate the faithful, honorable, spiritual work done by the "Anna's and Simeon's" of the church, but to point out that prayer needs government, as does the church.

In a large church, the pastor may delegate oversight of prayer, but he realizes that delegation is not abdication. The delegated person has the blessing and cover of the pastor and therefore operates under his anointing. Of course prayer pastors, as with all appointed leaders in the local church, must not be novices, but need to meet the qualifications for leadership just like any pastor as set forth by Paul in Timothy. Training is always part of the process, so the Pastor who has been delegated oversight in the domain of prayer also needs to feed and train those under him in the "how-to's" of prayer. In our church as the senior pastor I set the structure of domain prayer before our congregation. However maintaining awareness of and fervency for prayer is the responsibility of our prayer pastor and those she is training and has delegated her authority to.

Unless prayer is led supernaturally, it can become a system of works and legalism. For prayer to be powerful it must be spiritual and be led supernaturally. Most people don't pray because they want to, but because they are directed and led to. As with Stephen, prayer leaders should be selected for their good reputation, they should be "full of the Spirit and of wisdom," so that they can be "put in charge of this task" (Acts 6:3). They should be, "...full of faith and of the Holy Spirit" (Acts 6:5).

As pastors and faithful leaders take up their roles in the spiritual guidance of prayer, they will be enabled to operate incisively in their domain. When a leader is appointed to his domain, the word of wisdom, the word of knowledge and the ability to operate in tongues and interpretation accompany his post. As the domain leaders are trained, they become skillful at discerning the guidance of the Holy Spirit and in directing the corporate gathering to accurately visualize the goal, intensively verbalize the objective, as well as to *pray through* or persevere with all manner of prayer. As we have begun to raise more leaders in the domains, one of the results of this empowerment is that the depths in our ranks of leaders has begun to grow. We have "...committed these teachings to faithful men who will be able to teach others also" (2 Timothy 2:2 NKJV).

If prayer is going to be effective pastors cannot allow themselves to become too busy for prayer, nor can they avoid being personally involved in prayer. Pastors are God's agents to model prayer and show what it means to be a prayer warrior. They are not meant to be policing attendance, but inspiring participation. In order to call people to pray, and pray in the power of the spirit, we must understand this is a spiritual exercise, not just a religious chore or a social gathering. Many churches have prayer meetings which are at best nothing more than a gathering to pray in a scattered manner without a plan or preparation, or at worst, are merely a time of fellowship with coffee and donuts.

My experience has been that when we make prayer our business and then get down to the business of prayer, we get the results we are looking for.

As I write this book we are having a prayer revival of sorts. We just finished an extended time of prayer and fasting, followed by an all night prayer meeting where more than 2,000 people participated. Our morning domain prayer attendance has increased to the largest it has ever been and would be larger if our nation was not suffering from fuel and transportation problems.

The most powerful dynamic of domain prayer is that we do not only recognize the pastoral gift ministry, but also the other five-fold ministry gifts in each domain area. For instance we have a man who is a banker, but he is also both apostolic and prophetic in the financial realm. The five-fold ministry extends the Kingdom of God beyond the local church when men and women are released into their domain to function as reformers. Reformation must be led by apostolic leaders in each sphere. I believe I have men and women who are apostolic in the areas of education, medicine and government, and in fact every sphere in the market place. These people must be recognized in the church as leaders in their own right. Although they may not carry governmental authority in the local church, they carry great authority in their domain.

It is critical for every senior pastor to understand that there is a difference between a good leader and a kingdom-thinking, purpose-connected leader. Every leader that a senior pastor delegates, must be connected to God's call for that ministry. When that connection is in place, then leaders have no difficulty laying down their lives, their time and their money to fulfilling the kingdom vision. As the senior pastor recognizes, positions and directs these leaders, their effectiveness will increase exponentially and they will find fulfillment and fruitfulness. These expressions of the five-fold ministry in each prayer domain serve as a model and encouragement to others, to also direct their God given gifts and talents into further expressions of God's Kingdom. Gradually over time, things begin to happen. God has the blueprints for reformation, but we must trust God and respond to His direction. As we get involved in our respective domains, so we will advance personal transformation as well as national reformation.

Right and Wrong vs. Life

A key aspect of keeping prayer alive pastorally and in keeping with the mandate of reformation, is that there must be attention given to how prayer is framed. We must focus on life core values as opposed to right and wrong core values. Jesus Himself says, "It is the Spirit who gives life; the flesh profits nothing. The words that I speak to you are spirit, and they are life" (John 6:63 NKJV).

Many well-meaning believers have been caught up in a downward-leading spiral of *right and wrong, either-or, black and white* thinking. This has crept into the church and manifests itself in the attitudes, prayers and lifestyles of many in the church. This kind of thinking is destructive in every way. When people start thinking along these lines in prayer, they soon devolve into judgment and comparison. They soon have *right and wrong* ways to pray, they soon have *right and wrong* prayers and so often end up like those people fasting in Isaiah 58.

...Yet on the day of your fasting, you do as you please and exploit all your workers.

Your fasting ends in quarrelling and strife, and in striking each other with wicked fists. You cannot fast as you do today and expect your voice to be heard on high.
                                    Isaiah 58:3,4 (NIV)

This kind of thinking goes back to the time of Adam and Eve in the garden. God told Adam and Eve they could eat of any tree in the garden, except for the tree of the knowledge of good and evil. Adam and Eve and all mankind suffered because Eve led Adam into partaking of this tree. Mankind has a propensity for wanting to judge everything by the standard of good and evil, or right and wrong. This tends to polarize people and take them away from their focus and purpose. In our prayer meetings we have found that *either-or, right-wrong, black-white* thinking brings death, but *both-and* thinking brings life. This all-inclusive kind of thinking can help a pastor or prayer leader keep prayer focused, effective and alive.

Unchecked this *right-wrong* kind of thinking can grow into an attitude that says, "We are the church with the best praise, the purest doctrine, the cutting edge programs, and the other churches are not *with it*. This kind of thinking will keep us divided from the work of God in the cities and nations we find ourselves in, and will bring division to the overall vision of God. We cannot say we are right and everyone else is wrong. There is no right church and wrong church. I always tell our church, if you're looking for the perfect church, when you find it don't join it, because you'll mess it up!

God wants all His fullness to dwell in Christ and if we are in Christ all His fullness should dwell in us. God is more interested in us eating out of the tree of life and embracing people and life-giving ideas than in trying to be judges of others' prayers, thoughts and actions. This does not mean I'm against calling sin, *sin*, but I have seen the church marginalize so many people in the name of *right* and *wrong*, or *sinfulness*, that was neither. For example, it wasn't too many years ago, that to be a business person in the church meant you were probably crooked at best and evil at worst! Somehow we wanted the business person's money, but not to be tainted by the secular connotations and judgments that the church generally had about business people.

I have found these judgments in almost every one of the prayer domains. For example, somewhere along the line government became *evil* and God was *good*. Why can't both be *OK*! Many of our young people thought that to be involved in politics or government would keep them from being effective for God! We teach that to be effective for God in government and politics you must be involved. How can the church think it can effect change without being a part of the process, is not wisdom, but is eating out of the tree of the knowledge of good and evil! We need to be, "filled with the knowledge of his will through all spiritual wisdom and understanding" (Colossians 1:9 NIV).

In my early years of ministry there was such an emphasis on divine healing that if someone went to a doctor, or worse yet considered becoming a doctor, they were considered "anathema." This *right and wrong* thinking led to the confusion of many.

When Jesus gave the five-fold ministry gifts, the purpose was so that the members of the body of Christ would attain the "whole measure of the fullness of Christ" with the purpose in mind of building each other up in the love of God.

> ...until we all reach unity in the faith and in the knowledge of the Son of God and become mature, attaining to the whole measure of the fullness of Christ.

> Then we will no longer be infants, tossed back and forth by the waves, and blown here and there by every wind of teaching and by the cunning and craftiness of men in their deceitful scheming.

> Instead, speaking the truth in love, we will in all things grow up into him who is the Head, that is, Christ.

> From him the whole body, joined and held together by every supporting ligament, grows and builds itself up in love, as each part does its work.

> **Ephesians 4:13-16 (NIV)**

Jesus Himself was the best example of *both-and* thinking. The Pharisees, Sadducees and lawyers of His day were always trying to catch Him out with *right and wrong* thinking, but He would always respond with *life*.

> [One day the Herodians and Pharisees banded together and asked Jesus], **"Tell us then, what is your opinion? Is it right to pay taxes to Caesar or not?"**

But Jesus, knowing their evil intent, said, "You hypocrites, why are you trying to trap me?

Show me the coin used for paying the tax." They brought him a denarius,

and he asked them, "Whose portrait is this? And whose inscription?"

"Caesar's, they replied. Then he said to them, "Give to Caesar what is Caesar's, and to God what is God's."

When they heard this, they were amazed.

Matthew 22:17-22 (NIV)

Jesus never bound Himself to right and wrong thinking, thus He could operate in a dimension that today many in the world are still seeking for: that is the dimension of wisdom.

So, we have concluded that there are basic principles that govern what it means to be someone who operates in life and wisdom, they can be summarized as follows:

- Both doctors and divine healing are acceptable.

- Both God and government are okay.

- Both business and church are necessary.

- Both education and the Bible have their place.

- Both financial and spiritual organizations are needed to support the vision of the Kingdom of God.

- Jesus is the way, the truth and the life. The way to the truth is through life.

- The Church is to serve, upward, inward and outward. We need to reach out in all directions. We are not limited to just one expression of worship.

- We accept Jesus both as the gentle lamb and as a lion.

It's our job to reform our domains. We do not want to be critical and judgmental, *right-wrong* thinkers. Our mandate is to bring our spheres of influence back to God's way of life. We want to be a Church of life givers in the image and likeness of God the Father, Who loves to give good gifts to His children (Matthew 7:11), Who is rich in mercy (Ephesians 2:4 NIV).

Testimony: Fidelia Gandiya

Fidelia Gandiya's testimony is one of the most powerful I have heard, as a manifestation of the Father heart of God and His supernatural provision, bringing life to Fidelia and her family, where everything appeared set to bring death.

Fidelia shares her story:

Christmas of 2003 is a day that will forever remain imprinted in my mind, although the dark cloud has since left. It was the day when we buried my husband of 15 years. At only 41 years and with no previous known history of disease he had passed away, leaving me widowed with four children including a nine month old baby.

Was I angry and bitter with anyone and with God? No! But definitely the foundations of my life had been destroyed. I clung to the words of one preacher during the funeral, "I needed to build new foundations if I was to go on and to successfully raise my children." Isaiah 54 and Psalm 125 were then, and still are, my bedrock scriptures and they helped me to walk through the season of my grief.

The death of my husband also happened at the time when I had just moved from where I had been fellowshipping to join my husband and family at Celebration Church. I was therefore very humbled when Pastors Tom and Bonnie Deuschle, who did not know who I was then, sent me flowers and a card and even called me and my family to the pastor's suite to pray for us and encourage us. At that point we supernaturally had a father restored to our family and have always since then looked to Pastor Tom as our father.

One of the early teachings I got from Pastor Tom when I came to Celebration Church was on first fruits. I knew about the tithes and offerings, but had never heard about the first fruits. The revelation was 'mind boggling' and to me, since obedience is always better than sacrifice so I immediately committed myself to bringing in my first fruits. So when I got a promotion as a Finance Director two days after the death of my husband, I committed myself to giving my whole first salary. Questions flew through my mind, of how I would manage without my husband's support, and with no salary to pay the fees and all other family needs as a single parent, particularly at the start of the year. But when I referred to the scriptures on first fruits I noted that if I bring the first fruits to the man of God, and he prays for me, my whole harvest will be blessed. This helped me to decide to give. Pastor Tom prayed for me and from there on the blessings that I received were absolutely amazing.

To begin with, I was told that in my new position, as part of my conditions of service, my school fees would be paid for, my fuel allowance would be unlimited, home security was provided and all phone bills paid for. These are the things my husband used to do and God had immediately restored each of these areas. We were overjoyed and praised God as a family for this. But God was not done with me yet, in fact it was just the beginning.

Towards the end of January 2004, I received an email from the CEO of Econet, the company my husband had been employed by. In this email the CEO promised that I was going to receive my husband's salary for six months, complete with all of the benefits he had been receiving, like fuel and a free telephone line; just as if my husband was still employed! God's faithfulness was overwhelming. As if that was not enough, he promised to pay all my children's fees including the baby until they are through with school. Two sets of school fees! This was too much, but that's my God, my maker, my husband; everything was coming in double portions!

One of the prayers I had made to God was for my children and I not to wander in grief or wallow in "a pity party" forever. The Holy Spirit came through and we were all comforted. For me especially, I had a new experience with my fellowship with God. I used to be one of those skeptics who would role my eyes if anyone said God spoke to me. God proved me wrong. He spoke to me so much, during prayer, at night, during the day and always. My journals and study Bible is full of God's assurances and promises, most of which happened and some of which I am still standing in faith and hope.

Having tasted the fruits blessings and joys of first fruits, I began 2006 by sowing my first fruits as well. True to Himself, God humbled me again and again. Needless to say, I ended the year financially in a place of overwhelming abundance when my family receives 125,000 worth of Econet shares that year. Who me? Yes, I Fidelia, was wealthy! I used the bulk of the shares to build my family mansion, which is almost complete now. The rest is still in the form of shares as my children's inheritance.

Bringing first fruits to the man of God has become my lifestyle. In 2007 the lines once again fell for me in pleasant places and God promoted me to a job paying in foreign exchange. The voluntary retrenchment package I got from where I had worked for 20 years included buying a vehicle for ZWD46,000, which was approximately US$10.00! Yes, there is no mistake! For a $50,000 bearer cheque I got a Nissan Hardbody. Bearer cheques are the major form of currency in Zimbabwe in this current economic crisis. Now you tell me that first fruits, tithes, offerings and sacrifices, iced with prayer do not work, and I will show you the evidence that it works.

Did I bring my first fruits to the man of God from my new job? Oh yes! Now I am waiting in hope for a blessed harvest enough to sponsor my daughter's education in America and to sow more into the Kingdom and to feed my family.

In closing I can declare that I believe that the keys of first fruits and prayer that Pastor Tom handed to me, is a treasure I will always cherish. My life has been revolutionized. Unless someone reminds me, "Fidelia you are a widow," and tells my kids that they are fatherless, we tend to forget because of what God our Father has done in our lives.

Chapter 9
Surgical Prayer is Practical

The critical point of this chapter is that Surgical Prayer is by definition practical. Of all the aspects of Surgical Prayer this is by far the most important and strategic. God is intensively and intentionally practical. In Genesis it is recorded that God worked for six days and rested on the seventh. Work entails exertion and effort, with the aim of producing something. Work is practical, not theoretical, and requires the expenditure of energy. The exceedingly large quantity of power required by God, to generate from nothing the entire world, is totally unimaginable. We can perhaps begin to appreciate a fragment of this from reading God's response to Job, in Job chapters 38-41. The intricate detail, the complexity of design, the dynamic interaction of every chemical process together with the interlinked and inter-related physical laws and elements that comprise the Universe in which we live, go beyond the beginning of our understanding. One of the greatest understatements ever is that God is the expert practitioner. We have no concept of someone who is effective in every intent of their thought and action.

In a world that for the most part has fallen far short of the idiom, "my word is my bond," we need revelation to comprehend that every word God speaks will achieve the purpose for which God spoke it. God says, "So shall My word be that goes forth from My mouth; It shall not return to Me void, But it shall accomplish what I please, And it shall prosper in the thing for which I sent it" (Isaiah 55:11). God does not operate on percentages of success, He is 100% successful in each endeavor He undertakes. This concept is totally foreign to us, particularly those of us who are used to talk, with little or no action. This does not reflect the character of our Father. If we become all talk, we run the risk of becoming, "clouds without rain, blown along by the wind..." (Jude 1:12 NIV). God's Word is His bond, so should our's be.

Suffice it to say, God is practical in character. Jesus illustrated this in His parable about the son who said he would work, and did not, versus the son who said he would not work, but did. The one who brought pleasure to the Father is the one who did the work!

How then can we credit God's character with the passivity of unanswered prayers. God interacts intensively with us. If our prayers are not being answered, this grieves God. What did Jesus say? You have not because you ask not, ask that you may receive. God is practical, He is action. He does not sit on His throne unengaged with his prize creation, but is this often the position we relegate God to in reality? What are we missing? Because God is missing NOTHING!

A patient will not undergo surgery unless something specific is practically done. A surgeon is paid to carry out surgery, which is a practical procedure, carried out by a highly qualified practitioner, who is registered to practice.

Likewise in a war situation, there is also great cost entailed, a set procedure and very detailed planning which is carried out and then followed, with an extremely high degree of co-ordination and exceptionally precise communications, in order to execute "surgical warfare." Surgical warfare is intentionally and intensively practical.

By definition "practical" means; "Pertaining to practice or action. Capable of practice or active use; opposed to speculative" (Webster's Dictionary). That which may be used in practice; that which may be applied to use; "concerned with the practice, useful in practice, engage in practice, inclined or suited to action rather than speculation" (Oxford Dictionary). The Chambers Dictionary expands this to include; "engaged in doing something, efficient in action..."

The word "practice" is defined, "Frequent or customary actions; Habit is the effect of practice. Exercise of any profession; as the practice of law or of medicine. Frequent use; exercise for instruction or discipline." To use or exercise any profession or art; as, to practice law or medicine; To use or exercise for instruction, discipline or dexterity. To perform certain acts frequently or customarily, either for instruction, profit, or amusement; To exercise any employment or profession. A physician has practiced many years with success" (Webster's Dictionary).

Many Christians have not experienced successful prayer lives. In fact, if you ask most Christians how successful their prayer lives are, they will tell you, "probably not as successful as I pretend it is," and in some cases the ratio of answered prayer is very low. Part of the problem is, that we have a tendency to rationalize things. We say "I don't know why it didn't come right" and choose to not really think about why. We just keep on praying and praying and sometimes never even wonder what is happening. Occasionally we may speculate about the reason why our prayers have not been answered, and then reach an impasse and just return to praying the same way as before.

I spoke to one young man who told me, "I used to pray regularly, until I came to the point where I stopped praying because I didn't seem to get answers any more. I thought I could do better by myself, if I went and did everything by myself. I thought I could just go there and do my own thing, because prayer didn't work. I began to revert back to some of my unsaved ideas. I used to think Jesus Christ was for people that needed a last resort. I used to think that praying was for people that needed a place to crash, to get stuff off their chest. I thought it was always good to talk to people but if you couldn't, you could just talk to God."

I have seen some people with an attitude about prayer that they are just going to throw a prayer out there, but they do not really believe that God is going to do much in response to their prayer. Others thought prayers had to be read out of a book. In fact before I received Christ, I also used to just read prayers or quote them from memory, but did not get any tangible results that I was aware of. I really just thought my prayers were to give homage to God, not actually to get any results.

I now realize that part of prayer is to give honor and praise to God, but God also wants us to realize that we can secure things on this earth for the good of His kingdom and for people through prayers. Jesus says, "Until now you have asked nothing in My name. Ask, and you will receive..." (John 16:24 NIV). God doesn't put any limit to it, he actually goes on to say, "that your joy may be full."

Something we are experiencing is just how much God delights in our audacious prayers, prayers outside of the box and outside of any realm of possibility, because it is then so obvious that the only way this thing could have happened, was because God Himself did it. One of the attributes that mark surgical domain prayer, is the fact that because it is so focused, we often see the answers to our prayers in the newspapers, news releases and magazines in the nation. Effective, productive and fruitful are descriptions of practical prayer. I encourage all who pray with us not only to bring issues that need to be prayed for from the media, but also to bring joyful reports when our prayers make a difference and they're reported in the media. With this kind of attitude you can imagine how exciting prayer can become. These prayers on a national level and corporate level spill over into people's personal lives and when it comes time for testimonies at cell level our cell groups are nothing short of dynamic.

There are many Christians worldwide who have the saddest faces. They are bent over with grief and act like it is so hard to be a Christian. How can we walk around like that, when we have a promise like this? "...ask anything that your joy may be full" (John 16:24 NIV)!

I heard a story about Smith Wigglesworth who was ministering at the turn of the century in England. He was a simple plumber and did regular jobs for a wealthy woman. On one occasion, the woman asked him how come he was just beaming with joy, and had a light shining from him? And he said, "this morning I woke up and my wife and I prayed for our two kids who were both sick with a fever, and they both got healed! So I'm just so full of joy. The joy of the Lord is my strength!" She immediately asked, "can I have that joy too?" This is the kind of influence we can all have.

How can you have joy when your bills are not paid and your family is sick? When you are depressed and your car is on empty, how can you have joy? How many of you have really prayed and asked God concerning a crisis in your personal life or in the nation? Have you seen any results? Christians, we are going to learn that our joy may be full. You see sometimes we act no different from people in the world. Sometimes we are the worst of the complainers, what hope does that give to the world?

I've heard of people praying for a national change of Government for 20 years and there's been no change. Doesn't that mean we should change prayer tactic or focus? One of the reasons for not looking at prayer answers is because we have accepted that God's answers to our prayers may be, "Yes, no, or wait!" These three answers to prayer that traditionally have been taught, I believe do not reflect God's character or principles as seen in the light of most scripture. God responds to expectant hearts, which are full of faith, with an attitude of trusting Him. When we expect a *no*, it gives us excuses for unanswered prayer, and a *wait* answer simply needs to be accepted. But to believe that we have the answer that we pray for, regardless of the time it takes to manifest, now this I believe is a joy to the heart of God.

Many philosophies have crept into the Church, especially concerning prayer, and we know that philosophy is not passive nor benign. One of the most deadly of these espouses that as humans we are helpless, we either can't do anything ourselves, or we should not without the help of God. Another is that there are forces arrayed against us that are so diabolical that we are helpless against them. At best we should avoid them and at worst appease them. Are we that helpless? Have we no role to play in the outcome of the affairs of life? Study the principles of Scripture. Everything that God does is based on a pattern according to principles. Many have abdicated their roles in politics, or business, or the media or entertainment because they feel these domains have been overrun by wicked people and evil. Many have gone into hiding or into denial. Some have begun to seek an "other-worldly" experience, almost a mysticism, while others are waiting for heaven and are just holding on for the end. The truth is, God hardly ever delivers His people from evil rulers. Instead, He prospers them in the midst of the evil ruler's empire. God is interested in our character and not where we live. We have lived and ministered 25 years here in Zimbabwe in less than perfect circumstances, but God has blessed and prospered us.

God is not delivering men or nations from bad Government, His pattern is to use men to influence national situations for His purposes, to bring blessing and deliverance. So why do we pray that God will deliver us from a bad government when it seldom happens? God's principle is that, "no weapon formed against us will prosper" (Isaiah 54:17 NKJV), so God Himself delivers us from the day of trouble.

Sometimes we become impractical and even unbiblical in our praying. We have tried to "bind all the demons in hell," when we do not have that authority or power. Nor is it according to the pattern or principle laid out in the Scriptures for us by God. Jesus did not confront every wicked force when He was here, how is it then that we should presume to do so. The apostle Paul was practical, he waged war spiritually, but went through natural processes like you and I, in order that the word entrusted to him would go forth. We read his report in Corinthians,

> **Giving no offense in any thing, that the ministry be not blamed:**
>
> **But in all things approving ourselves as the ministers of God, in much patience, in afflictions, in necessities, in distresses,**
>
> **In stripes, in imprisonments, in tumults, in labours, in watchings, in fastings;**

By pureness, by knowledge, by longsuffering, by kindness, by the Holy Ghost, by love unfeigned,

By the word of truth, by the power of God, by the armour of righteousness on the right hand and on the left,

By honour and dishonour, by evil report and good report: as deceivers, and yet true;

As unknown, and yet well known; as dying, and, behold, we live; as chastened, and not killed;

As sorrowful, yet always rejoicing; as poor, yet making many rich; as having nothing, and yet possessing all things."

2 Corinthians 6:3-10 (KJV)

There has also been a tendency at times in some church circles to label each other as being negative characters from the Bible, for example, "she is a Jezebel, He is an Absalom, he is a Saul." We need to be very clear, these people appear in the Bible and were real people, but their stories were their own. Although they were probably trafficking in spirits, no one, especially a believer in modern Christianity, is Korah, Cain, Saul or any other spirits that we so glibly attach to others. A common label has been the *Jezebel spirit*. Well, there may be a *Jezebel spirit*, but the fact is, these simplistic labels have been pasted onto spiritual problems ad hoc without dealing properly with the root cause of whatever problem is now manifesting in *Jezebel-like* behavior. Like all sin, if unrepented of, it will cause harm. We are not to destroy one another, but to address the problem for deliverance and restoration for the individuals.

As we study these characters, the Bible says that they are given as examples for us and we must study them for the sake of the principles we can learn, especially in governing and guiding our own lives. Every human is prone to the sinful traits that we see in these characters. The point is: all these characteristics of every one of these demonic historic figures is latent in each one of us. What matters to God is that we deal with the issues in our hearts and walk in truth and faith.

In domain prayer time we don't emphasize prayer for individuals. The primary time scheduled for individual needs to be met in our church is in the cell structure and at the end of public meetings. Corporate time in prayer is intended to accomplish the large breakthroughs needed for each domain to advance.

After this, the Moabites and Ammonites with some of the Meunites came to make war on Jehoshaphat.

Some men came and told Jehoshaphat, "A vast army is coming against you from Edom, from the other side of the Sea. It is already in Hazezon Tamar" (that is, En Gedi).

Alarmed, Jehoshaphat resolved to inquire of the LORD, and he proclaimed a fast for all Judah.

The people of Judah came together to seek help from the LORD; indeed, they came from every town in Judah to seek him.

2 Chronicles 20:1-4

All the men of Judah, with their wives and children and little ones, stood there before the LORD.

Then the Spirit of the LORD came upon Jahaziel son of Zechariah, the son of Benaiah, the son of Jeiel, the son of Mattaniah, a Levite and descendant of Asaph, as he stood in the assembly.

He said: "Listen, King Jehoshaphat and all who live in Judah and Jerusalem! This is what the LORD says to you: 'Do not be afraid or discouraged because of this vast army. For the battle is not yours, but God's.

Tomorrow march down against them. They will be climbing up by the Pass of Ziz, and you will find them at the end of the gorge in the Desert of Jeruel.

You will not have to fight this battle. Take up your positions; stand firm and see the deliverance the LORD will give you, O Judah and Jerusalem. Do not be afraid; do not be discouraged. Go out to face them tomorrow, and the LORD will be with you.'

"Jehoshaphat bowed with his face to the ground, and all the people of Judah and Jerusalem fell down in worship before the LORD."

2 Chronicles 20:13-18 (NIV)

Is this not a good prophesy! "See the salvation the LORD will give you, O Judah and Jerusalem." Jehoshaphat sent forth people to praise; the outcome of this was that the enemy destroyed themselves. They didn't even leave one survivor. God's people spent three days gathering the spoils. From this day onwards, nobody ever came against Jehoshaphat. There are three things I want you to learn out of this passage!

We have to realize that to have command and charge over an area, means the enemy can still come and fight against you. God has given us supremacy over the carnal activities of this world. This is the time that the church should realize this. The spiritual weapons that Jehoshaphat used were:

- Collective fasting united prayer. He gathered all Judah together to pray.
- Public worship.

When we use these we will see the same result. This does not take away from what I have been saying, that the gathering together isn't enough if the prayers we are going to pray are unspecified and scattered. We must be determined to be surgically accurate and powerful.

I have tired of hearing churches make city wide announcements about reforms and revivals and how the nation has been transformed and changed with very little evidence in the lives of the average person in the city or nation. Whereas the Word of God says, "If my people, who are called by my name, will humble themselves and pray and seek my face and turn from their wicked ways, then will I hear from heaven and will forgive their sin and will heal their land" (2 Chronicles 7:14 NIV). Will prayer heal our land or will healing come as we take dominion in the areas that affect the areas of life. Prayer must move us to action. Any prayer that is a substitute for action is dead and impractical.

There may be times that the only thing you can do is pray. Prayer for people and individuals is powerful. However prayer for nations, without our corresponding engagement in our spheres of influence, without getting our hands dirty and even losing our lives or spending time in prison, makes the domains impotent. As people gather, strategies can form. Resources will be marshaled as the needs are revealed and understood.

When the righteous prosper, the city rejoices; when the wicked perish, there are shouts of joy.

Through the blessing of the upright a city is exalted, but by the mouth of the wicked it is destroyed.

Proverbs 11:10,11 (NIV)

There are so many aspects of this type of prayer that still need to be explored, and there are still so many blind spots in our lives and bad habits that we have learned that keep us as individuals and the Church from seeing the effects of our prayers, but I believe that if we practice and grow in the principles set forth in this book we will soon have not only surgical prayers, but powerful answers being manifested wherever we take up the call to Kingdom, Domain prayer.

Dr. Wazara has led the Domain Prayer for the Medical Domain since its inception and has taken up the challenge to bring about reformation in the field of medicine and its delivery. We are seeing many wonderful answers to our prayers in this domain, but as you will see in his testimony it overflows into every area of his life.

Testimony: Dr. Matthew Wazara

As a surgeon, I appreciate the precision of the art. God himself uses surgical terminology in dealing with nonproductive or malfunctioning body parts e.g. "cut out sinning eyes or amputate sinning limbs." The analogy of prayer being carried out in a surgical manner resonates very much in my spirit and its results have been remarkable in my domain, in my family and in my life as an individual.

Pastor Tom has taught us an approach to prayer which has been dubbed "bunker busting". As with surgery, the outcome is envisaged before the procedure. The one on whom it is performed shuts out all other influences, such as doubts and fears which are anaesthetized, and they are fully convinced of a favorable outcome. The prayers' act now as if he has already received what is being prayed for. All terminology is in the present and completed tense and not in future hopeful possibility.

Kingdom Principles Applied
Ensure Sustainability of Provision

The provision of sound medical services is a key in the development of any nation. The world's medical systems have failed whenever they have been driven by profit only, without a consideration of the staff that work in the medical service arena, the population to be served and without ownership within the industry. As a part of Kingdom reformation Pastor Tom has taught us that it is the Church's mandate to heal the sick, and so the delivery of medicine should be driven by Kingdom principles. In this way medical skills are retained, those needing medical attention are served, those funding this delivery make a living, ensuring the systems endure for generations.

To this end we have embarked on a delivery system in whose fullest expression will be a medical school, several hospitals and clinics and a medical insurance system. The reformation in the medical domain, will be evidenced by the fact that this system will be set to world class standards while situated in one of the world's most disregarded nations. To date we have been working seven years to advance this vision, and have received medical equipment towards setting up the system. We have researched, networked and hosted many short-term medical missions. We have experienced many advances, been crushed by many retreats, but understand that reformation is a process, and one to which we are committed. Pastor Tom says, "perseverance outlasts persecution," so although we have already been working to advance our Medical Reformation Vision for seven years, and we understand it may take a lot longer as it is a road we have never walked before, it is a process we will never give up on. I am privileged and excited to be a part of reformation and the extension of the Kingdom in the Medical Domain.

Chapter 10
Conclusion

I have had an urgency in me to get this God-given strategy to you, "His word has been in my heart like a burning fire shut up in my bones; I was weary of holding it back, And I could not" (Jeremiah 20:9). After God had spoken to me and said, "What I want in prayer is surgical accuracy that is powerful," I wanted to teach the church how to pray surgically accurate and powerful prayers, *bunker-buster* prayers. Since then, there has been a spiritual pressure compelling me to get the job done.

Having taught this progressive message for some time now, I am now seeing the start of an apostolic people rising, from key sectors in the nations, with a biblical world view, radical faith in God's promises and principles, and a passion and purpose to influence every sphere of life with the Kingdom of God.

From being in a place where the task of reformation has seemed impossible, the dawn is breaking. Although we are positioned in a nation with the fastest shrinking economy and the highest inflation rate in the history of the world, to name just a few of the *impossibilities* here, transformation feels like trying to eat an elephant! So how do you eat an elephant? One bite at a time! Real change takes place one person, one day, one prayer at a time, this is how we see the power of God make the impossible possible.

Determined to be voices of change and not just echoes in our society, has required a resolve that began with a decision, but has had to continue by persistent, daily application of the Word of God to our lives. Our vision of reformation of the nations, by "Building People and Building Dreams, Transforming Lives and Reforming Nations" is gathering momentum through daily application of surgical prayer, both individually and corporately.

Duplicity, that is, being one thing privately and another thing publicly or being something in the Church and something different in the world, has both diluted and negated the power and influence of the Kingdom of God in the world. When the Church is as immoral as the society it is trying to reform, our voice is lost, and we are no longer salt and light. We've seen that transformational development is a dynamic process, and that the society we are in will only change as individuals within that society change, and nations will then be discipled one person at a time.

Of one unshakable conviction I am utterly certain, that The Word of God stands and will deliver all that it says, though the world will be shaken. Right now across the earth the world is being shaken. There is a global shaking of national economies, of the nations' food stability, fuel stability and their national security structures. Even that which we all assumed unshakable is demonstrating a global shift from the usual patterns, the climate! This world is shaking, but The Word of God stands and will stand. As we form cultures with a Biblical world view they will be used to transform nations with opposing, hostile world views. As we apply godly wisdom it will lead us to be architects of reformation in blatantly pagan nations. What the Church has to offer is unique and given to us by God. We have access to wisdom from above. The church has an opportunity to give real answers to the world using a source that is inaccessible to the world, the wisdom of God.

One of the most profound effects of domain prayer is seen when we come together in our domains, we experience the power of purpose, because we all are focused on the same thing, and agreed as touching one thing, and subsequently see an increase in the intensity of God's power. The power of corporate prayer meetings is often, "destroyed for a lack of knowledge" (Hosea 4:6) or conversely established by the effective, maintained communication of the vision. Communication of the vision must be directed as many people don't pray because they want to, but because they are lead to. We realized the incredible dynamic brought about by the expression of the five-fold ministry in each domain, recognizing apostles, prophets, evangelists, pastors and teachers in each sphere. Unless prayer is led supernaturally, it can become a system of works and legalism.

Leading supernaturally releases corporate revelation, which is necessary for corporate prayer and corporate practice of the Kingdom! The source and director of the corporate revelation is the person who has been appointed by God to head your church, the man of God. Pastors are God's agents to model prayer and show what it means to be a prayer warrior. The principle that the man of God leads the church and casts the vision takes on more and more importance, and as the church applies this pattern, God releases His blessing and the vision advances.

Although we are fully aware of the problems we face, as we are surrounded by them on a daily basis, when it comes to surgical prayer, we choose to look for the heavenly picture of how it should be. Jesus said, "Thy kingdom come, Thy will be done on earth as it is in Heaven." How is it structured in heaven? What is the heavenly pattern? What is it that you see? We have to operate by faith in order to bring what is in the spirit, into reality. We begin to call those things that are not, as though they are. Understanding this is critical to accomplishing what God has tasked us to do in our domains. "It is God, who gives life to the dead and calls those things which do not exist as though they did" (Romans 4:17).

It is imperative that the Church once again begins to engage in not only speaking about and preaching about the Kingdom, but demonstrating the Kingdom. My experience has been that when we make prayer our business and then get down to the business of prayer, we get the results we are looking for. It is easy to pray, but challenging to act practically and reformationally on what we've prayed. In this way our prayers not only speak to the problems, but our actions are the answer to the prayers.

It is easy to obtain, but hard to maintain! It is easier to obtain the vision from God, than it is to maintain the momentum to bring it to pass. If we're going to maintain what we have advanced in prayer, we're going to have to work hard at prescribing frameworks and holding ourselves accountable to them. When we not only pray, but are willing to follow our prayers with sustained action, we will then preserve a measure of godly rule for the generations to come.

The legacy we leave as reformers is achieved by our willingness to use finances sacrificially to impact the areas and domains we are praying about. Until the level of sacrifice that we are willing to operate at exceeds the amount of sacrifice which our contemporaries are giving to ancestral spirits through spirit mediums and other witchcraft practices, we will not see the Kingdom established. Reformation and relevance do not come without great sacrifice.

As you finish reading this book, join me and thousands of others as they make a decision to realign themselves with those who lead in prayer and the vision for surgical prayer.

"Father God I repent for duplicity, for being an echo in my sphere of influence and for abdicating my responsibility to be your Kingdom influence to my sphere of authority. I also repent for seeking to live independently of Your corporate Body, the Church, and of your appointed leaders. Right now I decide to change.

I submit to the spiritual leaders you have placed over me. I commit to finding out the vision of our church from our leaders. I will daily speak these visions into being. I will daily speak precise, penetrating, purposeful, prescriptive, prophetic, pastoral and practical surgical prayers over my life, my family, my sphere, our church and our leaders. Amen."

Significant Statements

• May the Holy Spirit help you to lay hold of these practical and effective keys that have transformed my prayer life and have changed large numbers of my church members into a forceful army of intelligent, focused and surgically sharp intercessors.

• Although I could see tremendous value in the truths contained in all this material, only a handful of people were responding to the prayer concepts put forward. Why was this? This question would eventually lead me to change the way I think and feel about prayer, and eventually write what you are reading in this book.

• There seemed to be no prolonged strategy of prayer that could sustain a quorum.

• We now live in the day of surgical warfare. We can go in and we can surgically remove one person and leave the rest of the civilian population untouched.

• As I was watching, God spoke to me and said, "That's what I want in prayer, surgical accuracy."

• Once again I heard God say, "I want to teach the church how to pray 'bunker-buster' prayers."

• My intention was to empower the vision of our church, which is "building people, building dreams; transforming lives, reforming nations."

- God had given me a mandate to build a church, a family of believers, that would bring about transformation and reformation in Africa and affect the world, starting in Zimbabwe.

- We could no longer afford the luxury, or should I say deception, of being one thing in the Church and something different in the world.

- It was in this context that God spoke to me about raising up apostolic people from the key sectors of the nation with a biblical world view, radical faith in His promises and principles, and a passion and purpose to influence every sphere of life with the Kingdom of God.

- Instead of being a voice of change we have become echoes in a secular, humanist society.

- Transformational development is a dynamic process. Societies change as individuals change, and nations are discipled one person at a time.

- An integral part of this dynamic which we have encouraged is the expression of the five-fold ministry in each domain.

- Although the Kingdom of God influences natural governments, it is more a disposition than it is a structured government.

- Daniel and Joseph were both raised in cultures with a Biblical world view and were used to transform nations with opposing, hostile world views.

- Eventually Daniel and Joseph's godly wisdom led them to be architects of reformation in blatantly pagan nations.

- What the Church has to offer is unique and given to us by God. We have access to wisdom from above.

• The Church has an opportunity to give real answers to the world using a source that is inaccessible to the world, the wisdom of God.

• When we choose to engage in Kingdom rule there are positive, identifiable consequences. If we neglect Kingdom rule there are also negative, identifiable consequences.

• That's why I say that the Kingdom of God is a disposition, not a destination.

• Because God had given me this idea of domain prayer, when we came together in our domains, we experienced the power of purpose, because we all got focused on the same thing, and agreed as touching one thing, and have subsequently seen an increase in the intensity of God's power. We also encouraged the expression of the five-fold ministry in each domain, recognizing apostles, prophets, evangelists, pastors and teachers in each sphere.

• My experience is that the greatest warfare I ever face is trying to stay in right thinking, peace and joy, when those around me are in insanity, distress and fear.

• These prayers in fact, do not constitute prayers of the Kingdom. God cannot honor fear, doubt, anxiousness or for that matter any negative emotion.

• What happens? Something I'm afraid we haven't seen enough of in our prayer meetings. The place in which they prayed is shaken, they are all filled with the Holy Spirit, and they speak the Word of God boldly. Isn't this really what we are all looking for? To me this is surgical prayer.

• See when the Word of God comes to you, that becomes your decree.

• We have to operate by faith in order to bring what is in the spirit, into reality.

• You begin to call those things that are not, as though they are. Understanding this is critical to accomplishing what God has tasked us to do in our domains.

• What was really happening is I was seeing differently and I was decreeing differently.

• When you pray, you pray in faith, you begin to pray seeing what is done.

• I had noticed a trend that when Pastor Tom makes an announcement as our apostle, the authority he carries in this office causes his pronouncements to come to pass. It is as if the angels associated with his office are released with the speaking out of what it is God has mandated him to action (Pastor Nicky).

• Penetrating prayer results in "taking territory, and includes both strategy and perserverence."

• One of our key statements is, "perserverence outlasts persecution."

• The pertinent question to consider at this point is, has the church to date, persevered in application of the Word, to produce evidence of the rule of God, that can be broadcast to all nations and accurately convey who God is.

• Corporate revelation is necessary for corporate practice of the Kingdom!

• Part of being reformers is the willingness to use our finances sacrificially to impact the areas and domains we are praying about.

• Until the level of sacrifice that we are willing to operate at exceeds the amount of sacrifice which our contemporaries are giving to ancestral spirits through spirit mediums and other witchcraft practices, we will not see the Kingdom established.

• Reformation and relevance do not come without great sacrifice.

• Not all people in corporate prayer carry the same authority, either in life or in the spirit.

• Prayer has as much to do with the character of the person praying, as with the prayers being prayed, when it comes to the kind of prayer that will lead us to reformation and transformation of a nation.

• My goal was not to shame the young man but to help him base his life and his prayers in reality.

• "If you are a lizard in Zimbabwe, you will not be a crocodile in London." This is more important than anyone will ever know when it comes to prayer.

• "...instead we start visualizing and praying what the Kingdom of God looks like. Being fully aware of the problems, we choose to look for the heavenly picture of how it should be.

• Jesus said, "Thy kingdom come, Thy will be done on earth as it is in...as it is in Heaven." How is it structured in heaven? What is the heavenly pattern? What is it that you see?

• My passionate intention is to help people pray powerfully and effectively, because the more of this type of prayer that we all engage in, the more rapid the expansion of the kingdom of God will be.

• "What we see is what we attract."

• "Some people are trapped, not because they are evil, but because of judgments that are held against them."

• Remember a *bunker busting* prayer is spoken in the present tense, not the future. It is a detailed and energetic visualization of what we see existing in heaven and we know by faith will be realized on earth.

• Visualization is a vital step to answered prayer that is only surpassed by action.

• It is necessary for us to take stock of how we are praying and the results we are obtaining, and where appropriate, change the manner in which we are praying.

• In terms of specific results, guidelines for prayer act as a scaffolding ensuring that our specific prayers are built into lasting edifices.

• Their statement to Nebuchadnezzar was their affirmation that reflected their prayer and their faith.

• Now, when the church is as immoral as the society it is trying to reform, we have lost our voice, and we are no longer salt and light. This is where prescriptive prayer is so necessary.

• Because these men not only prayed, but were willing to follow their prayers with sustained action, they have preserved a measure of godly rule for another generation.

• One of the lessons that we have learned is that it is easy to obtain things, but hard to maintain. If we're going to maintain what we have advanced in prayer, we're going to have to work hard at prescribing frameworks and holding ourselves accountable to them.

• It is imperative that the Church once again begins to engage in not only speaking about and preaching about the Kingdom but demonstrating the Kingdom.

• All change starts from the inside out, one person at a time.

• The agency that God uses to bring about reformation on earth is man, filled with His spirit. Man must engage in follow-through for prayers prayed and prophecies.

• I've been unable to possess the land, because my trust was in my natural abilities and these tell me of every giant in the land. When I give and pray at a serious level, I have supernatural help and the giants disappear. [Jeff Mzwimbi]

• In this way their prayers not only speak to the problem, but their actions are the answer to the problem. This is truly prophetic surgical prayer.

• Speaking out to people of like-mind amplifies the power of the prophetic.

• The anointing for prophetic intercession always imparts the grace for endurance.

• Unity of spirit and a common purpose in prophetic again amplifies the power of the spoken-out Word of God.

• Altering the specific known word that God has given us to pray in and to action, is called projection. This is one of the greatest hindrances in ministry. When we allow our own opinions, desires, and wishful thinking, none of which is the mind of Christ, to start coloring and changing the known Word of God to us, we are modifying and qualifying what we pray and say.

• Corporate prayer meetings are often "destroyed for a lack of knowledge" (Hosea 4:6) or conversely established by the effective, maintained communication of the vision.

• It is essential for us to understand that it is easier to obtain the vision from God, than it is to maintain it both for leaders and for the people they serve.

• Most people don't pray because they want to, but because they are directed and led to.

• Unless prayer is led supernaturally, it can become a system of works and legalism.

• If prayer is going to be effective, pastors cannot allow themselves to become too busy for prayer, nor can they avoid being personally involved in prayer.

• My experience has been that when we make prayer our business and then get down to the business of prayer, we get the results we are looking for.

• Pastors are God's agents to model prayer and show what it means to be a prayer warrior.

• Every leader that a senior pastor delegates, must be connected to God's call for that ministry. When that connection is in place, then leaders have no difficulty laying down their lives, their time and their money to fulfilling the Kingdom vision. As the senior pastor recognizes, positions and direct these leaders, their effectiveness will increase exponentially and they will find fulfillment and fruitfulness.

• *Both-And* kind of all-inclusive thinking can help a pastor or prayer leader keep prayer focused, effective and alive.

• How the Church thinks it can effect change without being a part of the process, is not wisdom, but is eating out of the tree of the knowledge of good and evil!

• Jesus never bound Himself to right and wrong thinking, thus He could operate in a dimension that today those in the world are still seeking for: that is the dimension of wisdom.

• The Pharisees and Sadducees and lawyers of His day were always trying to catch Him out with *right* and *wrong* thinking and He would always respond with *life*.

• Everything that God does is based on a pattern according to principles.

• It is easy to pray, but challenging to act practically and reformationally on what we've prayed.

For More Information

Zimbabwe:

Celebration Ministries International

162 Swan Drive

Borrowdale West

Harare

Or

PO Box HG88

Highlands

Harare

+263 (4) 850880- 850892 telephone

+ 263 (4) 850 877 fax

www.celebrationmin.org

USA:

Hear the Word Ministries USA

P.O. Box 764707

Dallas, Texas 75376

htwmus@aol.com

To place an order, contact us at
Kingdom Celebration Music,

PO Box HG88 Highlands, Harare, Zimbabwe

Tel: + 263 (4) 850 880 -92

Or email us at kcm@celebrationmin.org

www.kingdomcelebrationmusic.com

Also available from

Hear the Music
and
Hear the Word Publishing

Affirmations: (CD's and Flash Cards) US$10 per set of CD and Flash Card

Authority, Blessing, Child of God, Children, Faith, Generations, Healing, Joy, Kingdom of God, Peace, Praise, Prosperity, Wisdom, Worship.

"These words which I command you today shall be in your heart. You shall teach them diligently to your children, and shall talk of them when you sit in your house, when you walk by the way, when you lie down, and when you rise up." The washing of the water of God's Word over you brings everything you need for life and for your life: Pastor Tom and his family have taken time to compile Old and New Testament Scriptures around the themes mentioned above. As you listen to the Scriptures the effect in your heart is LIFE CHANGING! As you declare them for yourself using the Affirmation Flash Cards you will see your life transformed.

African Rain: Sounds of Worship (CD) US$15

Nothing penetrates your being like the sweet smell of rain lingering in the arid African atmosphere.

This album will reach into the driest parts of your spirit and bring the refreshing you long for — and the Father longs to release into you — as we worship together.

All People of All Nations (CD) US$10

There is a phenomenon surrounding this album that truly depicts the nature of God. "And He has made from one blood every nation of men to dwell on all the face of the earth". "All People of All Nations" reaches across denominational, cultural and ethnic boundaries to offer a message of hope and encouragement to anyone who has ever faced a trial or temptation."

Building People, Building Dreams by Tom Deuschle (book) US$15

You have a dream, but have you built it? Tom Deuschle shares the faith and failure, adventure and agony, success and sorrow of the walk that God has led him through. The practical principles in this book provide an action plan for you to impact your own nation for Christ— and expand the borders of the kingdom of God in your area of the world.

Change The World (CD and DVD) US$29.99

The African Enchantment. Group power and dynamite hits you as the sound of this, the most recent and most dynamic praise and worship album is released into our airwaves!

Don't Give Up: Bonnie Deuschle (CD) US$15

Supernatural and anointed encouragement flows out of this album to lift you from where you are to where you can be in the spirit. The title track is on Out of Africa.

Great Connection, The by Bonnie Deuschle (book) US$15

"When the cry of praise covers the earth, Heaven will be shaken and My Son will come!" I believe Bonnie's book is going to be used in a mighty way to help bring this about." Mary Colbert, Mary Colbert Ministries

"My awesome experience with the uncommon prophetic music ministry of Pastor Bonnie has practically demonstrated the revelation that praise and worship is evidently the real atmosphere of miracles." Apostle Gbenga Igbafen.

Kingdom Series: Tom Deuschle (2xDVD) US$25

This ten-part series releases the revelation life of the Kingdom of God, to a world jaded by self preoccupation and independence. "Everything Jesus did is in the context of the Kingdom of God. As you allow the Kingdom to come, you begin to see God do something awesome in your life."

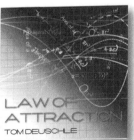

Law of Attraction by Tom Deuschle (DVD) US$15

Pastor Tom Deuschle unfolds the secrets of attracting the things you desire to yourself using the laws of the Kingdom of God. This popular teaching is a two-part series that has assisted many, not only to find their hearts desire, but attract that desire to their heart and lives.

Out of Africa (DVD) US$15

Featuring the awe-inspiring anthem, "Our Zimbabwe," set amongst breathtaking vistas and timeless scenes of our beautiful Zimbabwe. Also includes "Don't Give Up," "Sarah's Song," a favourite of children all around the world, and "Tambira," the message that takes Africa by storm.

Out of Africa: Africa Connection (DVD) US$15

A unique blend of sound styles and cultures, 'Out of Africa: Africa Connection' is an never forgotten experience.
Featuring; "Friend Like You", "Toimba Ishe", "Sold Out" and "Mary's Lamb", and including a fun "Special Features"

Out of Africa: With You, With Me (DVD) US$15

Featuring 'With You With Me" with Oliver (Tuku) Mtukdzi, this the third DVD in our 'Out of Africa' series touches deep and reaches wide, including "Praise 7", "Jesus I wake up for you", "Behold the Lamb" and "With You With Me".

Silver Collections: Bonnie Deuschle (CD) US$15

Songs spontaneously flow from this prophetic life. They are inspired, incisive, seasonal in the life our people and nation and influencing lives beyond the borders of our country. As Bonnie sings, an incredible anointing flows from her to powerfully touch the lives of those under the sound of her voice. Come discover this astounding artist and woman of God and her loving Shepherd Jesus Christ, through this amazing musical pilgrimage.

This is Our Story (CD) US$15

Generational inheritance impacts your spirit as you listen to this album packed with the authority of breakthrough for our generations and for the nations.

Zamar Worship (Instrumental CD) US$15

The music of '*Zamar Worship*' is a collection of instrumental versions of some of our most anointed worship songs. Zamar is a Hebrew word meaning, "to touch the strings or parts of a musical instrument, to make music accompanied by voice, to celebrate in song and music to God."

Order Form

Product	Qty	Price
Affirmations: (CD's and Flash Card Sets) US$10		
African Rain: Sounds of Worship (CD) US$15		
All People of All Nations (CD) US$10		
Building People, Building Dreams (book) US$15		
Change The World (CD) US$15		
Change The World (DVD) US$15		
Change The World (CD & DVD) US$29.95		
Don't Give Up: Bonnie Deuschle (CD) US$15		
Great Connection book US$15		
Kingdom Series: Tom Deuschle (DVD) US$25		
Law of Attraction: Tom Deuschle (DVD) US$15		
Out of Africa (DVD) US$15		
Out of Africa: Africa Connection (DVD) US$15		
Out of Africa:With You, With Me (DVD) US$15		
Silver Collection: Bonnie Deuschle (CD) US$15		
This Is Our Story (CD) US$15		
TOTAL ORDER		

Prices do not include shipping and handling

Name_____

Address _____

Telephone _____

Email_____

Credit Card _____

Exp. Date_____ Security Code _____

Kingdom Celebration Media

P.O. Box 764707 • Dallas, Texas 75376 US • kingdomcelebrationmusic.com